The Greatest Sniper Stories Ever Told

Edited by Tom McCarthy

Guilford, Connecticut

An imprint of Rowman & Littlefield

Distributed by NATIONAL BOOK NETWORK

British Library Cataloguing in Publication Information Available

Library of Congress Cataloging-in-Publication Data

Names: McCarthy, Tom, 1952– author.
Title: The greatest sniper stories ever told / edited by Tom McCarthy.
Description: Guilford, Connecticut : Lyons Press, [2016]
Identifiers: LCCN 2016006142 | ISBN 9781493018581 (pbk.)
Subjects: LCSH: Sniping (Military science)—History. | Snipers—History. | Snipers—Biography.
Classification: LCC UD330 .M39 2016 | DDC 356/.162—dc23 LC record available at
    http://lccn.loc.gov/2016006142

∞™ The paper used in this publication meets the minimum requirements of American National Standard for Information Sciences—Permanence of Paper for Printed Library Materials, ANSI/ NISO Z39.48-1992.

Contents

INTRODUCTION

ON THE FACE OF IT, BEING A SNIPER SEEMS LIKE A FAIRLY BLASÉ OCCU-pation. Superficially, it actually seems safe. Hide and shoot. No strain, no personal sacrifice. It couldn't be easier, right?

Wrong.

This collection of stories should quickly correct that misapprehension. Snipers are among the most highly trained soldiers in any army. The process of becoming a sniper is difficult, and many if not most who try—soldiers who think their superior shooting and cool demeanors are enough to make the grade—don't come close to making it.

Here is how one graduate of the rigorous Navy SEAL sniper course describes the training:

"The SEAL sniper course is three months of twelve-plus-hour days, seven days a week. Ironically, it is not all that demanding physically. Nevertheless, it is extremely challenging mentally."

It is not shooting ability or physical strength, he writes, but *intellectual capacity* that matters most.

But remember that the physical challenges are nothing to scoff at. A sniper must be capable of sitting, frozen for hours, in the most uncomfortable positions. Heat, insects, snakes, and the call of nature must be ignored for the sake of the perfect kill shot. A sniper must be capable of stealth, to be able to move so slowly, so invisibly that an unsuspecting target is oblivious to the almost certain death that awaits.

Mentally, a sniper must possess laser-like and unimpeachable concentration. He must have a focus so intense that nothing can shift its lethal potential. A sniper must make acrobatic calculations in the microseconds it takes to line up and squeeze off a shot. He must make instantaneous adjustments when the wind shifts or the target moves.

And a sniper must realize that if he is spotted he is dead, as sure as the sun will set every night. Targets sought out by snipers and their comrades hate snipers.

Snipers have short lives and make extraordinary sacrifices. And they do so in silence and anonymity. And for the most part, they are not exactly exalted.

Being a sniper is not for everyone.

As one now-retired Marine sniper once remarked, "Everybody hates snipers until they go into combat."

American sniper Chris Kyle, whose account of his time in Iraq appears in chapter one, put it succinctly in an interview. Talking about the stuff that makes a good sniper, he said, "It's not just being a monkey on a gun— anyone can pull a trigger. . . . it's observing the area. Knowing the culture. Knowing exactly what's going on. Being able to pick out an oddity."

This collection will make crystal clear the extraordinary skills needed to be not only a steely-eyed shot, but also a total sniper—an invisible, robotic killing machine whose sacrifices have saved countless times the lives of their comrades.

Not much about what is required to be a sniper has changed over the years, as you will read about in stories from the Civil War through Afghanistan—from the Vermont sharpshooters chosen for their marksmanship to wreak havoc on the lives of Southern rebels to the trenches of World War I to Marines in Vietnam.

The men who comprised the Vermont sharpshooters, for example, were chosen only after many others were rejected because they did not meet exacting standards. That's how all snipers are chosen, and why they are truly elite. Here is what an officer in charge of selecting the sharpshooting regiment from Vermont wrote about the process:

> *To insure this it was ordered that no recruit be enlisted who could not, in a public trial, make a string of ten shots at a distance of two hundred yards, the aggregate measurement of which should not exceed fifty inches. In other words, it was required that the recruit should, in effect, be able to place ten bullets in succession within a ten-inch ring at a distance of two hundred yards.*

Here is just one snapshot of the rigors and the extraordinary shooting skills of these sharpshooters. At an exhibition in front of President Abraham Lincoln, one colonel in the Vermont regiment "fired three shots at different portions of the six hundred yard target; when having satisfied himself that he had the proper range, and that both himself and rifle could be depended upon, announced that at the next shot he would strike the right eye of the gaily colored target. Taking a long and careful aim, he fired, hitting the exact spot."

As these gallant sharpshooters would learn, and as many snipers in other wars from other generations would learn, being a good and stealthy shot does not necessarily mean victory. As you will read, the Vermonters paid a heavy price.

Nearly sixty years after the Civil War, the mystique of the sniper was still admired, even by adversaries. Snipers played a horrific role in the trenches during World War I. With British and German forces massed sometimes only hundreds of yards from each other, a quick shot from a skilled sniper could and did destroy lives and morale. In the early years of this trench warfare, the Germans held the upper hand.

As one British observer noted, lamenting the superior Germans: "The hunter spends his life in trying to outwit some difficult quarry, and the step between war and hunting is but a very small one. It is inconceivable that a skilled hunter in a position of command should ever allow his men to suffer as our men sometimes did in France. It was all so simple and so obvious."

Major H. Hesketh-Prichard, author of *Sniping in France*, was an analytical and talented man who was concerned about the heavy loss of life among British troops in the trenches. His thoughtful study of trench sniping not only improved British marksmanship, but, many believed, saved the lives of over 3,500 Allied soldiers.

He wrote:

The officers believed that when warfare became more open, he [the sniper] would be useless. This proved perhaps one of the most short-sighted views of the whole war, for when it became our turn to attack, the sniper's duties only broadened out. Should a battalion take a trench, it was the duty of snipers to lie out in front and keep down the German heads during the consolidation of their newly-won position by our men, and were we held up by a machine-gun in advance, it was often the duty of a couple of snipers to crawl forward and, if possible, deal with the obstruction.

It was also during World War I that concern for marksmanship and shooting prowess became paramount in the US Army. One officer writing in 1918 in the *The Plattsburgh Manual, A Handbook for Military Training*, an excerpt of which appears here, had this to say:

There's no more luck in shooting than there is in solving a problem in geometry, or in a game of billiards. It's all practice, nerve, and science. Ninety-nine out of every hundred normal, virile men are more or less nervous when they first step up for rapid fire. Practice and will power are the correctives. The most thrilling experience you will have at a training camp will probably come when you step up to the firing line on the target range to fire your first shot. The great majority of new men grow pale, become nervous, lose their calm and poise, while they are on the firing line. This is a fact, not a theory. And this loss of nerve is not confined to the new man. Any shot, however old and experienced, will tell you that he fully understands what we have just described.

There was trench warfare during the Korean conflict as well. And again, not much had changed in the ensuing years after World War I, and by further extension the Civil War. Snipers were valuable:

Gunny Mitchell had killed so many North Korean and Chinese soldiers on the frozen slopes of the Chosin Reservoir, all the way to Hagaru, that he had long ago lost count. Armed with a venerable M1-D sniper rifle, Mitchell and his spotter had terrified the hordes of Chinese troops sweeping up frozen ice ledges to attack the well-bunkered Marines. When an automatic weapons position needed to be neutralized or Commie leaders shot dead during an attack, Mitchell was always lurking beside the grunts' foxholes, picking his victims with a polished and discriminating eye.

You'll read more about him here.

Other selections will show that while the technology of death has improved to the point where a good sniper can make a kill shot on a moving target from 1,100 yards away, as Joe LeBleu does in "The Long Shot," some things have never changed. Targets are not personal, and the enemy must be eliminated to save lives.

Here is how one sniper recalls a kill shot:

"Putting the crosshairs on Mr. RPG's upper sternum, I squeezed the trigger. The bullet hit him right underneath his nose. People picture that when a guy gets shot, he flies backward, but the opposite is often true. The bullet penetrates at such a high velocity that it actually pulls the man forward as it goes through, causing him to fall on his face."

That's how it works, and that's how a sniper can walk away with a feeling of contentment for doing his job. Like a man on a time clock: Punch in, punch out. The job is done, the day is over.

This collection of sniper stories brings together some of the most amazing, terrifying, and ultimately compelling stories—inside stories recounting the rigors of war. This is a collection, I hope, that will give breath and life and spit to a group of soldiers revered by many as the ultimate warriors.

CHAPTER ONE

Down in the Shit

Chris Kyle

ON THE STREET

THE KID LOOKED AT ME WITH A MIXTURE OF EXCITEMENT AND DISBE-
lief. He was a young Marine, eager but tempered by the fight we'd been
waging in the past week.

"Do you want to be a sniper?" I asked him. "Right now?"

"Hell yeah!" he said finally.

"Good," I told him, handing over my MK-11.

"Give me your M-16. You take my sniper rifle. I'm going in the front
door."

And with that, I headed over to the squad we'd been working with
and told them I was helping them hit the houses.

⸺

Over the past few days, the insurgents had stopped coming out to fight
us. Our kill rate from the overwatches had declined. The bad guys were
all staying inside, because they knew if they came outside, we were going
to shoot them.

They didn't give up. Instead they would take their stands inside the
houses, ambushing and battling the Marines in the small rooms and tiny
hallways. I was seeing a lot of our guys being carried out and medevac'd.

I had been turning the idea of going down on the street over in my
head for a while, before finally deciding to go ahead with it. I picked out

one of the privates who'd been helping the sniper team. He seemed like a good kid, with a lot of potential.

Part of the reason I went down on the streets was because I was bored. The bigger part was that I felt I could do a better job protecting the Marines if I was with them. They were going in the front door of these buildings and getting whacked. I'd watch as they went in, hear gunshots, and then the next thing I knew, they'd be hauling someone out on a stretcher because he just got shot up.

It pissed me off.

I love the Marines, but the truth is these guys had never been taught to do room clearance like I had. It's not a Marine specialty. They were tough fighters, but they had a lot to learn about urban warfare. Much was simple stuff: how to hold your rifle as you come into a room so it's hard for someone to grab; where to move as you enter the room; how to fight 360 degrees in a city—things that SEALs learn so well we can do them in our sleep.

The squad didn't have an officer; the highest-ranking NCO was a staff sergeant, an E6 in the Marine Corps. I was an E5, junior to him, but he didn't have a problem letting me take control of the takedowns. We'd already been working together for a while, and I think I'd won a certain amount of respect. Plus, he didn't want his guys getting shot up, either.

"Look, I'm a SEAL, you're Marines," I told the boys. "I'm no better than you are. The only difference between you and me is I've spent more time specializing and training in this than you did. Let me help you."

We trained a little bit during the break. I gave some of my explosives to one of the squad members with experience in explosives. We did a little run-through on how to blow locks off. Until that point, they'd had such a small amount of explosives that they'd mostly been knocking the doors in, which, of course, took time and made them more vulnerable.

Break time over, we started going in.

INSIDE

I took the lead.

Waiting outside the first house, I thought about the guys I saw being pulled out.

I did not want to be one of them.

I could be, though.

It was hard to get that idea out of my mind. I also knew that I would be in a shitload of trouble if I did get hurt—going down on the streets was not what I was supposed to be doing, at least from an official point of view. It was definitely right—what I felt I *had* to do—but it would severely piss the top brass off.

But that would be the least of my problems if I got shot, wouldn't it?

"Let's do it," I said.

We blew the door open. I led the way, training and instincts taking over. I cleared the front room, stepped to the side, and started directing traffic. The pace was quick, automatic. Once things got started and I began to move into the house, something took over inside me. I didn't worry about casualties anymore. I didn't think about anything except the door, the house, the room—all of which was plenty enough.

—⁓—

Going into a house, you never knew what you were going to find. If you cleared the rooms on the first floor without any trouble, you couldn't take the rest of the house for granted. Going up the second floor, you might start to get the feeling that the rooms were empty or that you weren't going to have any problems up there, but that was a dangerous feeling. You never really know what's anywhere. Each room had to be cleared, and even then, you had to be on your guard. Plenty of times after we secured a house we took rounds and grenades from outside.

While many of the houses were small and cramped, we also made our way through a well-to-do area of the city as the battle progressed. Here the streets were paved, and the buildings looked like miniature palaces from the outside. But once you got past the façade and looked in the rooms, most were broken messes. Any Iraqi who had that much money had fled or been killed.

—⁓—

During our breaks, I would take the Marines out and go through some drills with them. While other units were taking their lunch, I was teaching them everything I'd learned about room clearance.

"Look, I don't want to lose a guy!" I yelled at them. I wasn't about to get an argument there. I ran them around, busting their asses while they were supposed to be resting. But that's the thing with Marines—you beat them down and they come back for more.

We broke into one house with a large front room. We'd caught the inhabitants completely by surprise.

But I was surprised as well—as I burst in, I saw a whole bunch of guys standing there in desert camouflage—the old brown chocolate-chip stuff from Desert Storm, the First Gulf War. They were all wearing gear. They were all Caucasians, including one or two with blond hair, obviously not Iraqis or Arabs.

What the fuck?

We looked at each other. Something flicked in my brain, and I flicked the trigger on the M-16, mowing them down.

A half-second's more hesitation and I would have been the one bleeding on the floor. They turned out to be Chechens, Muslims apparently recruited for a holy war against the West. (We found their passports after searching the house.)

Old Man

I have no idea how many blocks, let alone how many houses, we took down. The Marines were following a carefully laid out plan—we had to be at a certain spot each lunchtime, then reach another objective by nightfall. The entire invasion force moved across the city in choreographed order, making sure there were no holes or weak spots the insurgents could use to get behind us and attack.

Every once in a while, we'd come across a building still occupied by families, but for the most part, the only people we were seeing were insurgents.

We would do a full search of each house. In this one house, we heard faint moans and went down into the basement. There were two men hanging from chains on the wall. One was dead; the other barely there. Both had been severely tortured with electric shock and God knows what else. They were both Iraqi, apparently mentally retarded—the insurgents had wanted to make sure they wouldn't talk to us, but decided to have a little fun with them first.

The second man died while our corpsman worked on him.

There was a black banner on the floor, the kind fanatics liked to show on their videos when beheading Westerners. There were amputated limbs, and more blood than you can imagine.

It was a nasty smelling place.

After a couple days, one of the Marine snipers decided to come down with me, and both of us started leading the DAs.

We would take a house on the right side of the street then cross to the left and take the house across the way. Back and forth, back and forth. All of this took a lot of time. We'd have to go around the gates, get to the doors, blow the doors, rush in. The scum inside had plenty of time to get prepared. Not to mention the fact that even with what I'd contributed, we were running out of explosives.

A Marine armored vehicle was working with us, moving down the center of the street as we went. It only had a .50-cal for a weapon, but its real asset was its size. No Iraqi wall could stand up to it once it got a head of steam.

I went over to the commander.

"Look, here's what I want you to do," I told him. "We're running out of explosives. Run through the wall in front of the house and put about five rounds of .50-cal through the front door. Then back up and we'll take it from there."

So we started doing it that way, saving explosives and moving much faster.

Pounding up and down the stairs, running to the roof, coming back down, hitting the next house—we got to where we were taking from fifty to one hundred houses a day.

The Marines were hardly winded, but I lost over twenty pounds in those six or so weeks I was in Fallujah. Most of it I sweated off on the ground. It was exhausting work.

The Marines were all a lot younger than me—practically teenagers some of them. I guess I still had a bit of a baby face, because when we'd get to talking and for some reason or another I'd tell them how old I was, they'd stare at me and say, "You're *that* old?"

I was thirty. An old man in Fallujah.

Just Another Day

As the Marine drive neared the southern edge of the city, the ground action in our section started to peter out. I went back up on the roofs and started doing overwatches again, thinking I would catch more targets from there. The tide of the battle had turned. The U.S. had mostly wrested control of the city from the bad guys, and it was now just a matter of time before resistance collapsed. But being in the middle of the action, I couldn't tell for sure.

Knowing that we considered cemeteries sacred, the insurgents typically used them to hide caches of weapons and explosives. At one point, we were in a hide overlooking the walled-in boundaries of a large cemetery that sat in the middle of the city. Roughly three football fields long by two football fields wide, it was a cement city of the dead, filled with tombstones and mausoleums. We set up on a roof near a prayer tower and mosque overlooking the cemetery.

The roof we were on was fairly elaborate. It was ringed with a brick wall punctuated with iron grates, giving us excellent firing positions; I sat down on my haunches and spotted in my rifle through a gap in the grid work, studying the paths between the stones a few hundred yards out. There was so much dust and grit in the air, I kept my googles on. I'd also learned in Fallujah to keep my helmet cinched tight, wary of the chips and cement frags that flew from the battered masonry during a firefight.

I picked out some figures moving through the cemetery yard. I zeroed in on one and fired.

Within seconds, we were fully engaged in a firefight. Insurgents kept popping up from behind the stones—I don't know if there was a tunnel or where they came from. Brass flew from the 60 nearby.

I studied my shots as the Marines around me poured out fire. Everything they did faded into the background as I carefully put my scope on a target, steadied the aim on center mass, then squeezed ever so smoothly. When the bullet leapt from the barrel, it was almost a surprise.

My target fell. I looked for another. And another. And on it went.

Until, finally, there were no more. I got up and moved a few feet to a spot where the wall completely shielded me from the cemetery. There I took my helmet off and leaned back against the wall. The roof was littered with spent shells—hundreds if not thousands.

Someone shared a large plastic bottle of water. One of the Marines pulled his ruck over and used it as a pillow, catching some sleep. Another went downstairs, to the store on the first story of the building. It was a smoke shop; he returned with cartons of flavored cigarettes. He lit a few, and a cherry scent mingled with the heavy stench that always hung over Iraq, a smell of sewage and sweat and death.

Just another day in Fallujah.

The streets were covered with splinters and various debris. The city, never exactly a showcase, was a wreck. Squashed water bottles sat in the middle of the road next to piles of wood and twisted metal. We worked on one block of three-story buildings where the bottom level was filled with shops. Each of their awnings was covered with a thick layer of dust and grit, turning the bright colors of the fabric into a hazy blur. Metal shields blocked most of the storefronts; they were pockmarked with shrapnel chips. A few had handbills showing insurgents wanted by the legitimate government.

I have a few photos from that time. Even in the most ordinary and least dramatic scenes, the effects of war are obvious. Every so often, there's a sign of normal life before the war, something that has nothing to do with it: a kid's toy, for example.

War and peace don't seem to go together right.

THE BEST SNIPER SHOT EVER

The Air Force, Marines, and Navy were flying air support missions above us. We had enough confidence in them that we could call in strikes just down the block.

9

One of our com guys working a street over from us was with a unit that came under heavy fire from a building packed with insurgents. He got on the radio and called over to the Marines, asking permission to call in a strike. As soon as it was approved, he got on the line with a pilot and gave him the location and details.

"Danger close!" he warned over the radio. "Take cover."

We ducked inside the building. I have no idea how big the bomb he dropped was, but the explosion rattled the walls. My buddy later reported it had taken out over thirty insurgents—as much an indication of how many people were trying to kill us as how important the air support was.

I have to say that all of the pilots we had overhead were pretty accurate. In a lot of situations, we were asking for bombs and missiles to hit within a few hundred yards. That's pretty damn close when you're talking about a thousand or more pounds of destruction. But we didn't have any incidents, and I was also pretty confident that they could handle the job.

One day, a group of Marines near us started getting fire from a minaret in a mosque a few blocks away. We could see where the gunman was shooting from but we couldn't get a shot on him. He had a perfect position, able to control a good part of the city below him.

While, ordinarily, anything connected to a mosque would have been out of bounds, the sniper's presence made it a legitimate target. We called an air strike on the tower, which had a high, windowed dome at the top, with two sets of walkways running around it that made it look like an air traffic control tower. The roof was made of panels of glass, topped by a spiked pole.

We hunkered down as the aircraft came in. The bomb flew through the sky, hit the top of the minaret, and went straight through one of the large panes at the top. It then continued down into a yard across the alley. There it went low-order—exploding without much visible impact.

"Shit," I said. "He missed. Come on—let's go get the son of a bitch ourselves."

We ran down a few blocks and entered the tower, climbing what seemed an endless flight of stairs. At any moment we expected the sniper's security or the sniper himself to appear above and start firing at us.

No one did. When we made it to the top, we saw why. The sniper, alone in the building, had been decapitated by the bomb as it flew through the window.

But that wasn't all the bomb did. By chance, the alley where it landed had been filled with insurgents; we found their bodies and weapons a short time later.

I think it was the best sniper shot I ever saw.

CHAPTER TWO

Gunny Mitchell Comes to Casey's Aid

John J. Culbertson

ON FEBRUARY 15, 1967, OPERATION INDEPENDENCE WAS SECURED. SERgeant Casey, just out of the hospital, returned to An Hoa on limited duty. He was glad to see Ron Willoughby and the rest of his snipers, but deep inside Tom Casey knew that the Marines had to sharpen their infantry skills to defeat the Viet Cong and the stealthy North Vietnamese. Casey felt that his Marines were often too impatient to make a kill, and that they failed to go with the tide of events, taking what opportunities Charlie gave them. Forcing a quick shot usually meant missing the target and compromising the sniper's position without thinking out the next movement in advance.

The Viet Cong snipers, on the other hand, always had a secondary hide or escape tunnel set up to flee any Marine counterfire or artillery support, which would likely find their position after they opened fire. The VC also employed better camouflage techniques, using all natural plants and dyes to blend perfectly into their environment. The Communists were well-trained by older veterans who had done extensive combat sniping and understood the effect of creating diversions with explosive booby traps to confuse their prey and cover up the noise of their weapons. The Americans took an unreasonable pride in making the long shot ending in a kill. The Viet Cong snipers polished themselves on close-quarter surprise tactics when an American patrol was sighted. Only one man would be targeted and killed, walking around a bend in the trail or topping a rise on a hill. The Marine point would often be shot in the head. The Viet Cong marksmen never worried about leaving secondary targets alone while they concentrated their primary fire on the point scouts or the radiomen, who were easily identified in a Marine column.

As Casey pondered the logistics of getting his snipers further trained, a memorandum from 1st Marine Division came into Headquarters Company of the 2nd Battalion, 5th Marines:

GUNNERY SERGEANT VERNON D. MITCHELL TRANS-FERRED TO 1ST MARINE DIVISION TO HEAD UP DIVISION SCOUT SNIPER SCHOOL AT HAPPY VALLEY RANGE. MITCHELL RETIRED FROM THE MARINE CORPS IN 1964. HE IS A 1955 NATIONAL INDIVIDUAL RIFLE CHAMPION AT CAMP PERRY, OHIO. IN 1958 MITCHELL WON NATIONAL SERVICE RIFLE CHAMPIONSHIP IN THE U.S. COAST GUARD MATCH WHERE HE SHOT RECORD SCORE WITH 15 OF 20 BULL'S-EYES IN THE SMALLER "V" RING. MITCHELL IS A COMBAT VETERAN OF WORLD WAR II AND KOREA. HE HAS REENTERED ACTIVE SERVICE AT REQUEST OF CMC. GYSGT. MITCHELL REPORTS TO 1ST MARINE DIVISION HQ, DA NANG, FEBRUARY 1967, TO BEGIN ACTIVE SERVICE.
BY DIRECTION
HQ USMC
WASHINGTON, D.C.

It was like the Almighty had answered Casey's prayers by sending the Marine Corps' greatest combat sniper to Da Nang to teach his Marines the "real art of sniping." Gunny Mitchell had killed so many North Korean and Chinese soldiers on the frozen slopes of the Chosin Reservoir, all the way to Hagaru, that he had long ago lost count. Armed with a venerable M1-D sniper rifle, Mitchell and his spotter had terrified the hordes of Chinese troops sweeping up frozen ice ledges to attack the well-bunkered Marines. When an automatic weapons position needed to be neutralized or Commie leaders shot dead during an attack, Mitchell was always lurking beside the grunts' foxholes, picking his victims with a polished and discriminating eye.

In a story I related earlier, but which bears repetition, Gunny Mitchell's most famous encounter called for accurate shooting up a muddy slope when he and his partner were called to aid a confused U.S. Army unit that had bogged down under heavy enemy machine-gun fire. A distraught Army officer had all but given up any attempt to advance his unit due to strafing from an enemy machine-gun crew six hundred meters up a ridge. The North Koreans peppered his troops whenever they got out of their trenches to advance. Mitchell and his buddy took a few minutes to size up the situation, then asked the Army lieutenant to order some of his men to stand up and fire a few rounds at the enemy. The lieutenant took one look at Mitchell and his spotter, realizing they weren't bullshitting about their request. Mitchell and his partner snugged themselves into their rifle slings and as soon as the enemy machine gunners got their gun aimed and fired a long burst toward the Americans, the two Marine snipers squeezed their triggers one after the other, sending deadly bullets streaking uphill at the North Korean gunner and loader. The gunners' heads exploding horrified the Communist soldiers, who grabbed their packs and beat a frantic retreat up the hill and out of rifle range. Mitchell and his pal jokingly suggested it was likely safe for the Army to advance, but should they encounter additional enemy resistance, to please call first for assistance. As far as Marines were concerned, nothing compared to helping the United States Army out of the sorry-assed messes they continually stepped into in Korea. As Gunny Mitchell later always said, "Nothing fucks up a good war more than the Army! That's what Marines are paid to do—unfuck things!"

At their first meeting, Sergeant Casey knew that Gunnery Sergeant Mitchell had the experience in shooting, coaching, and, most important, in combat to create the kind of sniper school that would become a legend among the 1st Marine Division Snipers from the 1st, 5th, and 7th Marine Regiments. There would later be contingents of U.S. Army, Air Force, Navy, and Korean Marine Corps personnel who would attend the school to learn the principles of combat sniping prior to establishing their own sniper courses. Sergeant Casey had shot on the 2nd Marine Division Rifle Team at Camp LeJeune in 1964, and he knew what proper instruction standards were all about. Gunny Mitchell was still young enough, at forty-two years of age, to demonstrate proper firing positions and conduct live firing demonstrations for his students.

The first Marines Casey sent to the new Happy Valley school were the group of Fred Sanders, Dennis Toncar, Jim Flynn, Loren Kleppe, Vaughn Nickell, Ron Willoughby, and Tony Spanopoulos. Another team of newly arrived sniper candidates, including George Wilhite, Stanley Watson, Dave Kovolak, and Tom Elbert, would begin preliminary training under Sergeant Casey, going out on regular patrols and night ambushes around Hill 35. Casey was an expert at night ambush tactics, and he worked hard with his men to teach proper cover and concealment during dusk, just before nightfall, when the sniping is often the best. All told, he personally led some forty-eight night ambushes around the Chu Lai and Hill 35 Tactical Areas of Responsibility. His snipers learned instinctively to put themselves in the place of infiltrating Viet Cong sappers to realistically determine the likely avenues of approach, and then construct Marine ambush sites accordingly. As Tom Casey's father always said, "When the boys in the next pond are catching all the fish and you ain't, maybe you jus' picked out the wrong hole! If you can't beat 'em, join 'em."

Casey was a true field Marine with a quick, reasoning mind for warfare. Equating combat sniping in Vietnam with hunting squirrels and rabbits back home in the swamps and meadows of humid South Carolina, he knew the key to successful hunting was to be fully prepared and wait alertly along the trails where the game was moving. Vietnam was no different. However, Thomas Casey and his band of "13 Cent Killers" were the only Marine combat group that hunted the Viet Cong at night just as successfully as during the day. The VC hated the Marine night ambush operations because they denied Charlie the only time when he could move about with impunity.

When Fred Sanders, Ron Willoughby, and the rest of Casey's shooters arrived at Da Nang, they were trucked by six-by-six double-axle trucks to the Happy Valley Range next to the Sea Bee's rock quarry in the far western outskirts of the base. The 5th Marine Regiment snipers were issued the new Marine standard sniper rifle, turning in the old M1-D Garands of World War II and Korean War fame.

The new Remington Model 700 was a walnut-stocked, five-shot, bolt-action rifle with a match-grade, medium-heavy Douglas barrel. The trigger was a match Canjar setup with a crisp 2.5-to-three-pound pull. The walnut stock was uncheckered and cut into a modest Monte Carlo cheek piece that lifted the shooter's face up into the business end of a Redfield 3 x 9 power adjustable scope with an integral range finder that snipers seldom used in combat. Nonetheless, the Remington was a fine shooter, and after breaking in the bore, most sniper candidates could hold inside a one-inch, three-shot grouping at a range of a hundred meters. At three hundred meters, a good shot could cut three-inch-plus groups with Lake City Arsenal 168-grain match ammo. This level of accuracy might not win a match at Camp Perry or the Marine Corps base at Quantico, but the only marksmanship task in Vietnam was killing Charlie. That meant Casey's dingers had a target about ten inches from armpit to armpit. And maybe twelve inches vertically from the bottom of the throat down to the middle of the abdomen, to score a hit. Any Viet Cong or North Vietnamese who got holed by a 168-grainer doing over two thousand feet per second would have enough internal bleeding to water his garden back home. A chest-wounded VC would still have pools of hot sticky blood spilling out a wound channel big enough to stick a man's fist into or, to be anatomically correct, through the front of the sternum, bursting the heart before exiting out the back. Well, I think you have the idea. Any unlucky enemy hit by a .308 NATLO bullet in the chest or abdomen would be DRT.

Sergeant Casey came to the logical conclusion that much of the painstaking rifle range training that many Marines felt was gospel was overly scholastic. Formal training de-emphasized the realities that were life-and-death lessons in combat sniping and were not always encountered or addressed in range practice. Gunnery Sergeant Mitchell agreed. His "Rule number one" concerning engaging the enemy was that a sniper team would *never* engage any enemy unit that was too numerous for the snipers to quickly kill or to destroy their ability to fight. In other words,

Mitchell and Casey preached that if a sniper team scoped out a Viet Cong or NVA unit that was anywhere near platoon size or larger, then the sniper had standard orders (SOP) to call for air or artillery support.

The Marine Corps had foolishly allowed some legends to continue unchallenged. Fantasies about single snipers who engaged large NVA units and killed them all with a bolt-action rifle and a spotter armed with an M-14. These remarkable Marines were supposed examples of gallantry under fire. However, as Gunnery Sergeant Mitchell often said, "Combat is about the 'Marine team,' and not about individual heroism." Any sniper team that fired on a company of enemy troops would be killed, absolutely, in less than ten minutes.

It's true that examples of storied heroism make for fine boyhood reading, like the myths about Ulysses, Hector, and Achilles in ancient Grecian lore. But in Vietnam the encouragement of tactics like "solo patrols" or sniping large units by a two-man sniper team were the type of idiocy that got Marines killed in real battle. Was it any wonder that the personnel that encouraged these ridiculous acts had never been in combat? Their romanticizing ego drove them to misadvise young Marines who might die because they imitated these fanciful combat actions.

Gunny Mitchell and Tom Casey, two of the most experienced Marine combat snipers ever to draw a bead on the enemy, both urged their snipers to act aggressively but prudently in the field. Live to fight another day was the order to follow. If that didn't make perfect sense, then why did the Viet Cong always break away when the Marine firepower coned into their hideout and things got too hot to handle? There was no possibility of winning the Vietnam War by attrition, due to the availability of millions of North Vietnamese replacements, not to mention the reality that Communist Chinese troops had already been killed in combat along the Demilitarized Zone. China was capable of sending vast hordes of well-trained, fanatical troops to North Vietnam's aid. As General Douglas MacArthur had warned, "You do not engage in a full-scale land war in Asia and survive." Evidently the old saying, "One who fails to learn from history is destined to repeat it," was true and alive and well.

Mitchell and Casey both realized that the path to victory lay in fielding experienced Marine infantry backed by airpower, artillery, and well-supported by company weapons and dedicated sniper teams. Snipers are fully trained to function as a "combat multipliers" and would be working to extend the infantry arms capabilities, to annihilate the enemy by sowing terror and defeatism into his ranks.

Personal glory or heroic recognition has no place in modern infantry combat. Any great warrior will gladly tell a spellbound audience whose eyes are riveted on his Medal of Honor that there are always other Marines who were more deserving but unnoticed in the fire and hell of battle. All the great combat leaders—like Jim Kirschke, George Burgett, John Pindel, or the selfless savior of Operation Tuscaloosa, Jerry Doherty—will first praise the dying efforts of their unsung Marine grunts who do all the fighting and most of the dying. For years, Captain Doherty took much of the blame on his own shoulders for the blood spilled by Hotel 2/5 at the sandbar on Operation Tuscaloosa. But had it not been for Jerry Doherty's intrepid stamina and self-control under fire, it is likely that none of his men would have lived to fight again. As it was, Hotel 2/5 finally won the battle, if not the war. Many young Marines learned to appreciate the value of picking your ground and your battles carefully.

Gunny Mitchell and Tom Casey had the dual responsibility of training their snipers to be effective killers without encouraging them to throw their precious lives away in a stupid gamble to gain a moment's fame or their partner's regard. In Vietnam most of the heroes went home early—in a box.

Willoughby, Sanders, Toncar, Flynn, Spanopoulos, and tough little Vaughn Nickell split up into two-man teams to sight in their new weapons. The Remingtons were lighter than the M1-Ds by a couple of pounds, but the greatest surprise came in the optics used with the bold rifle. The old M1-Ds had a 2.5-power, side-mounted scope that gave modest magnification out to six hundred meters. The Remingtons with the Redfield variable 3 x 9 power tubes gave the Marines a firing capability out to a thousand meters. It was rumored that the longest single kill in Vietnam was made at over 1,700 meters—more than a mile—but I personally thought that was bullshit, unless the shooter had used the Palomar telescope to sight the enemy with. Anyway, the Remington turned out to be an excellent choice of weapon for a sniper rifle perhaps due to the synergy of its parts working together, rather than any one characteristic, such as a highly accurate barrel or smooth trigger. This is akin to requiring all the infantry elements of a Marine battalion, including the sniper unit, to work together in harmony. Incidentally, it's the meaning of the Chinese word "gung ho," or "to work together."

To familiarize themselves with the Remington, the snipers' targets were placed in a target butts at three hundred, six hundred, and a thousand meters. Willoughby, Toncar, Sanders, Nickell, Flynn, and Tony "the Greek" Spanopoulos went to work firing initial rounds to get on paper, then moving their elevation and windage knobs after each group of shots until they fired tight groups into the center black. Each shooter made single scratch marks on their elevation knobs to denote the correct setting for three hundred meters for actual fieldwork. Two scratch lines were etched on the elevation knob denoting a range of six hundred meters, and three scratch marks were cut to indicate a thousand meters. In the event that the snipers would fire in the winter rainy season, the bullet would fall more at each range than the normal, dry weather sight elevation. The snipers were instructed to hold off above the target to compensate for a lower bullet strike.

In combat, both Gunny Mitchell and Sergeant Casey emphasized practical tactics like "holding off" and "incremental holds on moving targets," instead of attempting to adjust or fine-tune the precision scope, which is unnecessary to accomplish the combat mission: "Seek out and kill the enemy with a well-placed shot." A well-placed shot has more to do with terrain, weather, wind direction and force, and sun glare or target illumination, than merely firing a set course on a rifle range. The great combat marksmen—like Mitchell, Casey and the rest of the 5th Marines' handpicked snipers—were all natural shots, and most were seasoned hunters and stalkers.

Gunny Mitchell used to laugh out loud at the constant questions about long-range sniping. He told the story about the young Marine who had shouldered his way through a thicket of bamboo, taking up a prone position and sighting some enemy soldiers in a village a half mile away. As he lay in his hide, his binoculars flashed beams of sunlight that painted the faces of the Viet Cong sitting around the open fire. A few minutes later all hell broke loose as VC bullets slapped into the grove of green bamboo from close range. The Marine had not heard or seen the Viet Cong crawl around his position until they could fire into his flank with their AK-47s. The Marine beat a hasty retreat back to his squad and, covered with sweat, told the awful tale of his near death. The Gunny smiled and said that the man's mistake was to not first alert his squad members. His second mistake was to sit in his hold instead of working in close enough to kill the Viet Cong. Instead, the Marine had gotten careless and by flashing his binoculars, advertised his whereabouts to the whole fucking village.

Mitchell stopped speaking and eyed the group of youngsters, all hell-bent on destroying the Viet Cong by themselves on their first day in combat. "Boys, just remember this Vietnam is an old country," he said. "The Viet Cong have lived here all their miserable lives. They haven't driven fancy cars around the countryside, they've walked every foot of it. They know this land a hell of a lot better than us. They'll find you ten times quicker than you can find them. Do not take unnecessary chances. The Marine Corps has spent a lot of Uncle Sam's money on your training. I hate to see good beer or good money wasted. *Never underestimate the Viet Cong! The sneaky little bastards will likely be here after we are gone.* Be patient and take the good shots they give you. Make the bastards bleed for their country, then all this Commie horseshit may not mean so much to 'em."

Everyone had a smile on his face, then began to realize that this little Asian "police action" might last a whole lot longer than anyone would have guessed. Getting yourself killed over some eager heroic stuff was just plain stupid. Ron Willoughby and Loren Kleppe, for instance, remembered that there would always be chaotic battles like the fight at the sandbar on Operation Tuscaloosa, where anybody could get his ticket punched for a quick flight home. Living often had a lot more to do with luck than skill. In the big battles, there was so much lead flying and mortar and rockets slamming into Marine positions that Lady Luck randomly selected her chosen survivors, while the Grim Reaper knocked over the fallen with the crooked nail of a twisted claw.

Along with the 0700 to 1700 hours of range practice, the "13 Cent Killers" of the 5th Marines had classes on camouflage techniques and wind-reading skills. After two weeks of intense range and classroom instruction they were ready for qualification at a thousand meters.

The shooters fired their Remington rifles at twenty-inch bull's-eyes, managing to keep all their rounds comfortably inside twelve inches. The Gunny had the personnel in the butts trenchline walk targets stuck on long stakes from left to right and then right to left at a quick-time pace, while the snipers practiced moving leads and holding or "trapping" leads on the targets.

Most shooters, including Vaughn Nickell and big Jim Flynn, soon learned that it was a lot easier to take a standard lead and move your sights along with the target than to pick a spot and fire, hoping that the target fell into a "trap" where the lead was already figured into the bullet strike. The more the young Marines fired their rifles from each position— kneeling to prone, sitting to kneeling, kneeling to offhand (standing), offhand to prone with a sandbag support at a thousand meters—the more they appreciated the ugly truths of combat. First and foremost, the reality is that you train for combat in battle—not on the rifle range. Second, shooters soon learn that there is no best position, but the terrain will dictate how you must fight. Third, the quickest shot is not necessarily the best shot, but the quicker shooter will kill the slower shooter—all things being equal. Do not fuck off on the battlefield! Take a good position, align sights, breathe and hold, squeeze the fucking trigger gently, recover and fire again. Fourth, the sniper who performs these functions without becoming overly emotional, but rather, more mechanical, allowing his rifle to kill the enemy, will come out the winner and live for another day. The neurotic sniper or frightened rookie who always hesitates to get a better sight picture or screws with his equipment will invariably die due to indecisiveness.

Personally, I believe that a true "13 Cent Killer" enjoys hunting the enemy so much that killing the prey is incidental to the stalk. Killing itself is painful in that it terminates the excitement of the hunt. A great sniper like Gunny Mitchell, Sgt. Tom Casey, Ron Willoughby, or Fred Sanders takes great satisfaction in stalking his quarry. When the target is finally in the sights, then the hunt is over, because the professional does not often miss. Killing completes the ballet, or perhaps the "dance of death." There is a certain sadness to it because it must be replayed to achieve that superlative high adrenaline rush that comes from taking another's life. The dance is only of true value when the opponent is as good or better than you are.

The final lesson that Gunny Mitchell conveyed to us was that the Viet Cong snipers were not just as good as us, but better. Why? Because they didn't get to go home! Vietnam was their home. Their only chance to live was to be ever careful and stealthy in moving, creative in camouflaging, and selective in killing. I had witnessed many Marines shot in the head at close range by Viet Cong snipers who took the easy, close shots and then melted into the jungle.

Few Viet Cong marksmen came out alive in protracted shootouts with the seasoned "13 Cent Killers" trained by Gunnery Sergeant Vernon D. Mitchell and led by Sgt. Thomas Casey. Out of all the skills the Marines had over the Viet Cong, only two stood out above all the others: exceptional shooting ability and indomitable courage and pride. These military virtues were the general hallmark of the United States Marine Corps in past wars and in tradition. These combat characteristics, like the battlefield heroics of wars long forgotten, were encouraged and revered by the two sniper legends, Gunny Mitchell and his favorite pupil, Sgt. Tom Casey.

CHAPTER THREE

It's Not About Killing, It's About Living, and Somehow I Lived

Lena Sisco

Looking at Marine Corps Scout Sniper Timothy LaSage, I couldn't help but wonder when he would get his own movie deal. Talking with him will make you think about life, fate, and luck; it will make you wonder how he's alive today to tell it.

Tim grew up in Sussex and Germantown, Wisconsin. He considered himself to be a good kid; he learned discipline at a young age from wrestling as a sport, he went to church on Sundays and had a Christian education that he felt positively shaped his morals and manners. He was polite and opened doors for people and said "Sir" and "Ma'am"; he was raised well. He also fit the stereotyped image of a young aspiring sniper. He had quite a unique opportunity to *"rough it"* when he hadn't even hit double digits in his age. His father, who was never in the military, was on a climbing team and went on rock climbing expeditions around the U.S. and would bring Tim and his older brother along on the climbing trips. They would pile in his old Datsun pickup truck and trek across the country to the Rocky Mountains, or wherever, where Tim, who was an 8-year-old at the time, would have to hike with his father, and his own pack, up to base camps (they were typically about five miles away).

They, along with the other climbers, would set up camp overnight so the next day his dad could climb while Tim and his brother waited for his return. There was no electricity and while his dad scaled rock cliffs with his team, Tim and his brother were left to fend for themselves.

His brother was two years older than him and ended up joining the army later on when he was in his late teens. At the age of sixteen Tim got lured into joining the Marine Corps by a recruiter because he could get in through an early acceptance program. So at seventeen years old, he was attending Marine Corps boot camp. He was eager, in good physical shape, and he also knew his way around rifles, shotguns, and pistols. As a kid he would duck hunt on the 500 acres of land that his family owned. He went through a hunter's safety course at the age of ten. He had never committed a crime so he had a clean record. He could have been the Marine Corps recruiting poster child. (You will see as you read his story, that's kind of what he is.) Upon successfully finishing boot camp he signed up for Marine Corps Security Forces and then after his first tour there he would go back to the Infantry.

While in Security Forces, Tim attended Basic Security Guard School, which doesn't sound too challenging, or sexy. But as a Marine Corps Security Force team member, *"you are not a mall cop, you need to have a security clearance so you can guard things like nuclear weapons."* After graduating Security Forces he was recruited for Fleet Antiterrorism Security Team (FAST) Company in 1993. Tim catapulted through his career in the Marine Corps, as you will see, from having a good base in mental and physical abilities as well as his expertise in handling weapons. FAST Company was one of the only special operations offensive units in the Marine Corps at the time since they fell under the control of a Navy Admiral. FAST Company Marines could deploy with Special Operations Command (SOCOM) elements because they went through special operations training in a sense; Marines in FAST Company got jump qualified, certified as Scout Snipers and in Close Quarters Battle (CQB) (how to clear buildings and neutralize any threats), and skilled in reconnaissance and surveillance.

Because Tim's shooting scores were top notch and he excelled at his physical fitness tests, he passed the Indoc (short for indoctrination) into FAST Company without a struggle. While in FAST Company he qualified with the Heckler & Koch MP5 9mm submachine gun (a weapon that is unique to FAST Company).

"FAST Company was definitely operational. The primary role of FAST Company is to recover Embassies that have been taken over. Nothing was really going on after 1993 and Somalia; it was kind of quiet until about 1997–98 outside of deployments to Haiti. During this time we remained active by deploying to England doing exchanges with the Royal Army (training in urban conflicts due to their missions against the IRA and other terrorist organizations), training in mountain warfare to include high angle shooting as well as tracking courses along with surveillance and deploying stateside. Some people raised their eyebrows and asked me how can you deploy within the U.S.? Well we did. We guarded nuclear subs when they were refueling or when they were dry docked and provided security in high threat areas such as around nuclear reactors, etc. It was an intense unit. Back in the early 90's we had the high tech pager for that time, and I remember being stationed out of Norfolk, Virginia, and we would be out at Hammerheads [one of the local dive bars that attracts a twenty-something crowd] in Virginia Beach at the oceanfront and our beepers would go off and we'd get called back to the command. It was our version of high speed." He laughs and so do I because I can picture him feeling "high speed" with his pager back then. "FAST Company was a great beginning to my career because it got me into advanced schools and training and a little bit of experience with real world assignments providing security."

He also got to work hand in hand with the U.S. Navy SEAL teams and Army Special Forces. After three years with FAST he changed commands. He left FAST in 1996 and moved over to 2nd Battalion, 4th Marines (2/4). While with 2/4 he deployed to Okinawa, Japan, and Australia for a Unit Deployment Program (UDP) where he trained constantly and honed his infantry skills. Upon returning from Okinawa he went on post-deployment leave and to pass the time he tried out for the Marine Corps soccer team, and made it. He played soccer every day and he met his wife, of seventeen years now, at the soccer field. He had to convince her that he was a Marine because all she saw was this guy who would arrive at the soccer field every day around noon, who was never in a uniform and never carried a weapon, who was never training or shooting, so she didn't believe it when he told her he was a Marine. All he did, she thought, was play soccer, so she thought that if he was a Marine, he sure had it rough. He explained that when Marines come back from a deployment overseas they usually get the first month off as leave. During the next six months you could be put into the Fleet Assistance Program (FAP) where you could get a job on base such as at the gym or with the Military Police, maintenance, etc. Infantry guys would be lent out to other units that needed help. After that you go back to your command again to begin training for the next deployment.

Playing soccer every day was great, but Tim would get bored with that quickly. To his surprise, he was asked to come up to the "1st Marine Division Schools" for his next assignment.

"In the Marine Corps you have three active duty Divisions and in those divisions you have a schoolhouse that can teach and instruct units on a formal level. There are many schools that can be taught there; however the normal schools are Scout Sniper Basic Course, MOUT—Military Operations in Urban Terrain, HRST—Helicopter Rope Suspension Training, and Mortar and Machine Gun Leaders Courses. As of now you will also find Reconnaissance Schools under the Schoolhouse as well."

He was a corporal at the time, one of the very few corporals in the Marine Corps who was not only allowed to, but asked to, teach other Marines, local Law Enforcement SWAT (Special Weapons and Tactics) teams, and personnel from Federal Agencies, in urban tactics and CQB. Carefree soccer days in the California sun were over. In 1998 he and his wife moved across country to Camp Lejeune, North Carolina, so he could be an instructor at SOI, training Marines who had just graduated boot camp. He was a student in that very same classroom not that long ago. He warned his wife, who was eight months pregnant with their first child at the time, that their lives would need to adjust slightly, well maybe significantly, to his new job. Back in California he had ample time to spend with her; now, he would be nonstop working and training; his life would be much more regimented. She was completely on board but it did take a little more of an adjustment than she thought. Tim was always in the field and she was stuck raising their child. It wasn't fun with him being gone over two weeks every month but at least he still was in the country, he would be home anytime he could, and he wasn't out of sight or out of communication, which she would soon experience in the future to a challenging degree.

After two years in North Carolina with Tim running around chasing and yelling at Infantry students, focused on his career, and her running the house and raising the family, she was ready for him to transition out of that unit. Tim admits she got the short end of the stick.

"She was a young mom figuring out parenting and she took that job on with no hesitation and gave it 100%, while I was working nonstop. I don't know how she did it. It was her show, her house, and I was a guest. I'd get hosed down outside sometimes before I was allowed inside. I usually spent my days yelling and screaming at students and apparently one night she says I choked her out while we were sleeping while yelling in my sleep for students to get into formation! We laugh about it now, but at the time she let me know that my behavior was, let's just say, not conducive to a family life. So I called my monitor up and told him to get me into any unit back at Camp Pendleton, just get me back over there in the Infantry!"

He soon left SOI off to his next set of orders, which were to the next deploying unit out of Camp Pendleton. It's the year 2000 and he is back in California this time attached to 2nd Battalion, 5th Marines (2/5). He checks in and 2/5 already had a deployment coming up.

"I asked the sergeant major, I was a FAST Company Marine, I'm a Scout Sniper, and instructor. Do you have any openings in the Sniper Platoon? He says 'awesome,' you have a lot of leadership. I'm sending you to Fox Company, which is a Boat Company, instead of a Sniper Platoon."

Even though it wasn't what he wanted at the time, that Company ended up being a great time and experience for him. He trained in Coronado, and was out on the ocean constantly, not a bad life. Being in a Boat Company in 2/5 you were always operational; we were on call for any piracy interdictions, water recovery operations, beach assaults on foreign soil, and any other Joint Task Force opportunities.

In 2001, before 9/11, Tim went on another UDP with Fox Company back to Okinawa, Japan. While there, 9/11 happened, the towers fell, and within days we packed up our stuff, boarded a ship, and were launched as a reactionary MEU (Marine Expeditionary Unit) per se. He was on LSD-42 with Team 5 of the Navy SEALs doing anti-piracy operations. "SEAL Team 5 was on our ship and we did some joint operations with them. We responded to a kidnapping of an American husband and wife by the Abu Sayyaf in the Philippines. The husband was killed during the rescue attempt but the wife was still alive. The Philippine Army was tasked with recovery after the initial attempt. We had to move on to East Timor to assist the U.S. Support Group East Timor with humanitarian and civic assistance projects. Being in a Boat Company we had the privilege to travel ashore, secure the hospital site we were assisting, and liaison with the SEALs; the Admiral came to see our progress."

When Tim got back to the States he got staffed out to augment the Military Police. After the 9/11 terrorist attack, all Military bases were at heightened security so there were 100% ID checks and vehicle searches, so the Infantry Marines helped man the gates. Tim went through a police academy to become an MP and therefore picked up his fourth MOS (Military Occupations Specialty). Tim was an Infantry Marine, Security Force Marine, Scout Sniper, Close Quarters Battle Team Member, Formal Instructor, and now a Military Policeman.

"It was special to be able to go through a police academy because I was certified in law enforcement skills and specific training. I got to work with the FBI when the government started a joint database tracking system where we would track all the 'wrong turns' onto military bases all over the country. Along with being a road unit I was able to apply my first responder abilities in highway accidents, domestic issues, and civilian unrest issues in the local community. Local police called us for support with immigration issues and deportation, and many instances of illegal narcotics citations issued to civilians who were searched when they accidently came onto base."

Near the end of 2002 Tim gets word that the Iraq invasion is getting ready to kick off. He is still in the FAP program since the Military Police extended him due to his training. The problem was he wanted to deploy to Iraq; he wanted to be a part of this invasion and would stop at nothing in order to deploy. His temporary command, however, had other plans for him. They had just invested all this law enforcement training in him and he earned the MP MOS so they wanted to keep him stateside. He knew there was no hope of them changing their minds so one day after work he just decided to check himself back into 2/5 on his own, who was eager to bring him back under their wing. There's a saying frequently voiced in the Military, "It's easier to ask forgiveness than permission," and Tim adhered to it.

In the Second Vehicle of the
U.S. Convoy Invading Baghdad

Tim got back into his unit, 2/5, just in time. They were set to deploy to Iraq in two weeks. He was anxious and somehow his wife supported his ambition. She was pregnant with their second child, Kenadie, and her husband was going off to war, not to man gates or patrol an ocean to thwart piracy, but to invade a country. It would be straight up combat. He tells me he feels bad now, but back then he spent those two weeks prior to going off to war at home watching war movies with the guys while prepping gear, sharpening knives, and getting into the mindset. (As he tells me this story, I think his wife must be a saint.)

On February 2, 2003, he landed in Kuwait. While over 100,000 U.S. forces were berthed in "tent city" (what the Military call a very large area of military tents), Tim and the guys in his Platoon dug holes in the ground roughly three kilometers south of the Iraq border; that's where they berthed, once his company left the tents. At the time Mike Cerre, a reporter from ABC *Nightline News* was following Tim's Company. They adopted his unit to shadow throughout the invasion. Americans saw war through the eyes of Tim's unit. While in tent city Tim got word that an independent Platoon was needed to detach from 2/5 and attach to 2nd Tank Battalion in order to protect the lead tanks from RPGs and small arms fire while the tanks engaged in tank warfare. Although Tim didn't necessarily raise his hand and volunteer, he secretly and eagerly hoped that he would be assigned to this special mission, and he was. Tim and his Platoon left 2/5 and joined 2nd Tank Battalion as a Division Reactionary Platoon. You may not know it, but 2nd Tank Battalion led the U.S. convoy in the invasion of Iraq as the lead of RCT 5 (Regimental Combat Team) and Tim's vehicle was the second in line.

On March 19, 2003, the president declared war on Iraq and Tim's platoon got word that they were pushing to the border. On the evening of 19 March, Tim's Lieutenant said to him:

"Sergeant LaSage, since we are the lead element we just got asked to go on foot via compass and patrol in the desert up to this grid and we have to leave in an hour."

Tim and his platoon (the Division Reactionary Platoon with Fox Company 2/5) grabbed their ruck sacks that had everything they were living off of stuffed inside and patrolled up to the border. Tim plotted the route and took point leading the Platoon of 40 guys. After digging holes for protection and waiting the next two days for the green light to cross the border, they finally jumped on an AAVs/Amtrak (Assault Amphibious Vehicle) for the invasion. The invasion was in four waves, or lines; the Army led one line and the Marine Corps led the other three. Sometimes the roads were too narrow so all four lines combined into one long line; Tim was in the second vehicle in that one long convoy of U.S. military vehicles. Think of a convoy that stretches from DC to Baltimore MD. There was one tank in front of him, all moving up to Baghdad.

"You looked behind you and it was miles and miles of military vehicles, you look in front of you and there is one. It was surreal."

Tim was truly at "the tip of the spear." According to the Huffington Post, 192,000 U.S. soldiers invaded Iraq that day.

"The biggest complaint for Recon (reconnaissance) and Sniper units during that time was that units didn't stop long enough to forward deploy us properly so we couldn't do our job, it was go, go, go all the time. I didn't have any complaints though because I was engaging the enemy on a daily basis for days on end without ever leaving that Amtrak."

While this convoy was making its way to Baghdad, there was no stopping; not to eat, sleep, go to the bathroom, or stretch your legs. The vehicles only stopped during those twenty-one days during the push to Baghdad to engage the enemy and refuel. There were anywhere between 18 and 30 guys inside that Amtrak with Tim, and more if they had to take Prisoners of War (POW) in the vehicle.

"There's about four guys on each side of the vehicle on top looking left and right. Everyone else is below, inside feeding you ammunition. It's packed. Since we only stopped basically to refuel, that meant we're in there for days. If you have to shit, you do it in an empty MRE (meal-ready-to-eat) bag while you are shoulder to shoulder with the guy next to you."

Tim laughs as he tells me:

"You're stuck doing it on someone else's lap."

I guess it is so gross and unbelievable you have to laugh. Once you do that, I can't imagine being too modest to do anything.

"If you get sick, you vomit in anything you can find while someone's crotch is in your face. It's not pretty. And you don't sleep. You may try to, but the adrenaline pumping through you from being constantly fired upon won't let you. The ten minute catnaps fueled the tiger."

Since there wasn't much space inside the Amtrak, they could only bring as much ammunition with them as they could fit. All the chairs were ripped out and the guys below sat on crates of ammunition. If they had to re-supply they had to wait until the convoy stopped so they could access the ammunition in other vehicles behind them. So when they engaged and killed the enemy they would collect RPKs (Ruchnoy Pulemyot Kalashnikova, a Soviet-designed hand-held machine gun), RPGs (Rocket Propelled Grenade, which is a shoulder-fired anti-tank weapon), and AK47s off the dead bodies killed in action and use their weapons as their "Recon by Fire" weapons. Recon by Fire was a war-time rule of engagement where we were able to engage dangerous areas without seeing the enemy. If they had to clear a room, they used their military issued weapons for precise surgical firing. Sometimes Tim and his Platoon would come across caches of weapons hidden in the ground and in staged pick-up trucks loaded down with weapons and they would collect them all or demo the cache.

As Tim is crossing the Iraq border, in the second convoy vehicle, preparing to invade Baghdad and engage in combat on 21 March 2003, his wife Jessica was back in Camp Pendleton giving birth to their daughter Kenadie. *People* magazine and the local Los Angeles news wanted to interview her because she just had a "war baby," but she declined.

Tim said, "She's not an extrovert by nature and didn't want to be bothered by the press and plastered all over the media. She just wanted to be with her healthy baby girls."

Tim wouldn't even know about his daughter's birth until three weeks later. A reporter for ABC *Nightline News*, came up to Tim, ripped off a little piece of notebook paper from his notebook, and handed it to him. On the paper it said, "6 pounds, 7 ounces, healthy," that's it. That's all he knew about his daughter and his wife for another couple of months. He had no way to communicate with her; she had no idea where he was or even if he was alive. She assumed he was because she knew the expected protocol, and the doorbell never rang with somber Marines in their service uniforms asking for Mrs. LaSage. I can't imagine just having a child, one of the happiest times for married couples and you can't even talk to your husband until months later. There is no sharing in the joy and stress of the first weeks of this new life. And to add to the stress, not know if you'll even have your husband coming home after the war, and if he doesn't, God forbid, he would have never got to lay eyes on the life he helped create that just came into the world. It's a sobering thought to those of us who don't have to go through that.

So while she was with their newborn child, Tim was getting shot at continuously from the mujahideen and fedayeen Iraqi fighters. They were usually shots from combatants on either side of the road from the convoy, who dug ditches and tried to fortify themselves or were hiding behind, on top, or in buildings. The tanks in the convoy were shooting at enemy armored vehicles, while Tim's main mission was to keep the "klingons" off the tanks. (Klingons referred to the Iraqi combatants who would rush the tanks shooting and try to climb on top of them to grenade them.)

The tanks were firing consistently. "If you've never been next to a tank when it fires, it blows your hair back even inside your helmet."

Tim engaged in a lot of close firefights. When the vehicles did stop, it was Tim and his Platoon's job to clear out all of the surrounding houses. He would jump out of the Amtrak and run to the houses they were next to, sweep the inside, take the weapons, and take the POWs sometimes.

At one refueling stop the convoy started taking fire. Of course, they were sitting ducks, and Iraqis started shooting at them from about 300 yards away.

"One guy is on a roof and one is in the doorway of the house facing us. My partner and I decide we'll each take one out simultaneously. As I squeeze off a round I see this white flash, and I look up and see a white SUV coming to a screeching halt on the other side of the highway; I hit the SUV. And now the guy on the roof is really laying down fire. He's about 310 yards away behind a three foot wall on the rooftop and he's ducking down behind the wall after every time he shoots. The stress of being the only two firing back at the enemy who was shooting directly at us was deterred by my partner making fun of me for missing initially . . . which I made up for on my second press of the trigger. The enemy fighter was struck in the chest and folded down below the roof wall that blocked our visual. I could see it was a solid hit and he would pass; however the thought of him being able to pop up and engage other Coalition Forces haunted me since I couldn't confirm his death. This happened often as we would engage the enemy while moving and we couldn't stop. We would see the hits on our enemies but it was so fast paced that you did not have time to verify or do 'dead checks' most of the time."

MY WIFE GETS A VISIT FROM BENCHMADE

The convoy is still on its approach to Baghdad. On April 4, six days before entering Baghdad, they were passing the vicinity of Azizyah. Tim and his lead vehicles came in contact with heavy enemy fire.

"This battle is later documented as the most significant battle against enemy conventional forces during this war."

Tim was shooting at the enemy in a field from right to left.

"I was shooting fast. As I hit the last guy I took what it felt like was a sledgehammer to my ribs and I fell down. I was expecting to see my guts hanging out. We are all wearing chemical suits at this time due to the Kurds being killed via chemical warfare the year prior and we still had the unknown threat of chemical attacks. I'm trying to reach inside my gear to feel around my ribs and scoop up whatever I think is coming out, and I feel something moist, but nothing sticky. I realize it's just sweat, no blood. What the heck I thought? I guess I'm OK. I looked at my flak jacket and it was ripped up on that side and my body armor was odd so I knew I was hit by something. A corporal was next to me, and he was laying there, his face was jacked up and he couldn't see through the blood. I cut his sling off his weapon, and stood back up. As I stand up we take an RPG hit to the vehicle. I take shrapnel fragments to the head and face from the RPG hit. I fell back down again, and I see only one Marine shooting out of the Amtrak. He was doing the Rambo thing up there going nuts on the enemy that were taking advantage of the lull in our fire. By now we had several Marines hit that have fallen into the overfull vehicle. One Marine was shot in the hand and oddly enough was laughing while doc was trying to wrap up what was left of his hand. Just about everyone that was outside the vehicle had been shot or took shrapnel. So I stand back up with a squad automatic weapon and grenade launcher and started working everyone out there, it was full on mayhem! We were supposed to go around Azizyah due to the known ambush waiting for us. When he got shot, we missed the turn and went straight into an ambush. It was rough. Picture a traffic jam and the first ten vehicles having to do a 19 point turn in a narrow street to get out of there and then drive back out of the city.

"It was pandemonium. I ran out of belt ammunition and grenades that day. I had shot all of the machine gun ammunition in that field and then I had used all of the HEDP (high explosive/dual purpose grenades). I found out I was out of grenades to shoot when a hand came up under-neath me from inside the vehicle with my next round and it's a green star cluster. One of the last enemy fighters during that episode popped out from a courtyard made of mud and grass. I ended up having to shoot at him with the green phosphorous. We all watched as the white circle that was at times closing off our consciousness due to heat, sleep, and food deprivation was stalled by the green burn of the enemy fading away from us. It was memorable to say the least. Driving back out of that city and firefight was surreal. I remember while we made our way back out and around that city it was almost peaceful as we drove. There was definitely time to reflect on those close calls as we CASEVAC'ed our wounded. The next firefight we had we ended up losing our First Sergeant. We knew before that we were not indestructible but to lose our First Sergeant made us feel a bit vulnerable.

"A few days after this firefight we were stopped because vehicles are refueling, and I write this letter to Benchmade knives. How the mail system works is that you write a letter on anything you can find, cardboard box, wrappers, and you put it in an ammunition can and send it back and pray that it gets to somewhere. So what happened earlier in that firefight when I felt the sledgehammer hit my ribs was that I got hit with an AK47 round in the ribs but it deflected off my Benchmade knife. The bullet penetrated the knife but it boomeranged it enough due to its heavy construction to where it hit the side of my body armor. If that knife didn't deter the bullet's path it would have penetrated my ribs and ricocheted around inside me against the inside of my body armor. God's will be done. I had a huge hematoma on my ribs with some lacerations. So I wrote Benchmade knives and tell them their knife saved my life. I had two knives in my hand before I deployed. My wife and I agreed that she would put one in her purse and I would take one to war. I took the Benchmade because it looked sturdy. Benchmade, like a Vietnam jungle boot, has steel on either side of the blade. I still have this knife with me today with a perfect hole through it.

"I send this story in an ammunition can and who knows where it went or if it would ever get to Benchmade. Well, it apparently got there. Benchmade is located in Oregon and when they received my letter their executives suited up, jumped on a plane and flew to my house where my wife was. I'm still at war and still haven't spoken to her yet. They wanted to present me with a new knife engraved with my call sign and she, having no idea of what happened, answers the door to see these men in suits with this knife they want to present to her now because her husband was shot! So she asks to read the letter I wrote, and mind you, I didn't hold back about what had happened to me since it was to a business and not my family. She reads about my near death experience in a firefight and the gore of war.

"Now, she's smart enough to know if I had been killed she would have been notified immediately, so she knew I was still alive, but in what condition? She had no idea. And I'm still in the fight while she's raising a toddler and a newborn by herself. I got a Purple Heart for that. I swore if I ever got hurt again I would be the one on the phone with her going into surgery so she wouldn't have to hear it from a stranger first. I never have taken Jessica for granted but I definitely have not made things easy for her. Having to have a stranger let her know if I was alive or not shouldn't be something she should have to go through. In fact, during a later deployment I called her one morning at 3am to tell her I was hurt very bad and was going into surgery to try to save one or both of my legs. When she heard the phone at that hour her heart must have stopped, but as soon as she heard my voice, she started to breathe again."

I tell him she must be a strong woman to be able to deal with that. She doesn't have a choice either. Tim agreed and even said he couldn't deal when his guys went on deployment without him, *"I get this gross feeling."* You have no communication with them but you are expected to be strong and go on with life just the same until they return, IF they return. That is a hard position to put people in and yet it's done, with consent, all the time. No matter who is left behind *"to keep the home fires burning"* they have a very challenging responsibility.

When the convoy neared Baghdad on April 9, the four lines of the convoy split to cordon off the city. Some lines went northeast across the Diyala River toward Saddam's Palace, some went to the Baghdad airport, and others went south to positions flanking the city. Tim was sitting outside Saddam's Palace under an overpass after completing a link up with the Army's 3rd Infantry Division. They were watching jets do bombing runs from his Amtrak. Tim doesn't remember to this day when or if he ever fully slept from 21 March to 10 April. He was always up top in the Amtrak and always awake. He took cat naps, but there was no sleeping.

They finally got to exit the Amtrak and enter Saddam's Almilyah Palace where possibly two American hostages were held. Before taking the city over, intelligence would report that Tim's Platoon missed Saddam by only hours when the units were in the vicinity of the Iman Abu Hanifah Mosque.

I Wore the Marine Corps Flag like a Superman Cape

Tim is now in Baghdad on the day our nation saw Saddam's statue being pulled down by U.S. Forces. At this time 1st Battalion, 5th Marines (1/5) got themselves in a pickle. Tim and the 40 guys with him in the

Division Reactionary Platoon were launched to go help 1/5 who were caught in an enemy reinforcing ambush. Tim's Platoon took three tanks and two Amtraks, supporting 1/5, to go after the enemy. This was the first time in history since the Vietnam War that the U.S. was engaged in tank warfare.

They came upon a choke point where the enemy was reinforcing their ambush site against 1/5; there were three tanks in an alleyway with the lead tank shooting down the street at enemy technical reinforcing trucks, and the middle tank was stopped in a junction of other alleys with the rear tank in trace.

"Iraqis are firing at them from tactical vehicles like something civilians have seen from Somalia. The main tank got stuck in an alleyway. It was banging its turret left to right and ends up knocking a light pole down which lands on top. All the rubble from the surrounding buildings being hit with the tank turret, gunfire, RPGs, grenades, machine gun fire, and concussion from friendly rockets being fired falls onto the tank and suffocates the turret mechanism. So this tank was completely stuck. The second tank was about 10 yards behind this tank and stops in the middle of a kill zone; there were a bunch of alleyways that met up and that tank was pinned down by heavy RPG fire, and soon that tank is ineffective since the street is too narrow to traverse the turret. We were engaging the enemy so we instructed the tank crew to stay inside since the volume of fire was impossible for them to get out. The third tank is stuck in last place and it can't go anywhere or assist the others."

So Tim and the guys go out on foot. They are in a huge firefight that lasted for eight hours, while on the other side of town the media is filming the celebration of the toppling of Saddam's statue.

"People had no idea there was a full scale battle going on, and I was in the middle of it. It was a crazy Hollywood scene. The enemy was trying to take the tanks, we were shooting at guys four stories above us, guys were throwing grenades at us that were going right across the bow of our tank into nearby yards, RPGs were hitting walls but didn't detonate, it was absolute mayhem for eight hours."

Tim reaches the guys in the downed tanks on the tank phone (there is a phone in the back of the tank) to see who's alive.

"The guys in the tank were shaken up, the enemy were running amuck outside; this was war! The guys in the tank told me they called in for air support. I can't talk to aircraft because we didn't have the same frequency in our ground troop radios. So I asked the guys in the tank who they called and they respond 'Somebody and we told them we had downed tanks and we need aircraft for support.' So I asked them, 'Did you tell them we were still here?' They replied, 'No. They said they are rolling in A10s for support.'"

Concerned and mildly frantic, Tim asks them, "Do you know what A10s are made for?"

Tim explains to them A10s are designed to take out tanks. Tim hangs up the phone and uses the turret for protection from the enemy fire while still engaging enemy and avoiding the burning car that was twenty feet away. Through the entire invasion Tim had been carrying a Marine Corps flag inside his flak jacket and another Corporal with him, Corporal Bradley, had been carrying an American flag; they gave them to each other back in the states prior to going off to war. They both take out their flags; Tim proudly wears his like a Superman cape and Justin proudly waves his in the air because of what they thought was going to happen, which luckily didn't, while they are on the turret of a tank still shooting at the relentless fedayeen fighters and taking enemy heavy fire. Not more than two minutes after they had taken their flags out, leaning over the turret to see down the alleyway, shooting at people, the first A10 comes in strafing right off of their bow and into the alleyways.

"All you hear is the glorious roll of the 30mm cannon on the A10 rolling above you. He takes off in a high pitch and rolls out and everyone is in awe. Guys start laughing and cheering while still engaging the enemy that has now exposed themselves more to hide from the overhead fire. I start to laugh and yelled out in a pre-victorious bark 'DASH 2!.' The second A10 rips through the other side of us raining casings on us. It was the whole nine yards, and wipes out a ton of dudes on either side of us. I would be remiss if I didn't recall the tank commander during this. At one point during this intense long battle I looked over at the lead tank and witnessed the officer out of his turret using a rifle over the alley wall at enemy fighters right to his side. Once he put the rifle down and drew his pistol we ran over to the front to support his firefight. It was quite intense and the volume of enemy and gunfire was uncountable. War historians state that over 100 fedayeen were killed during this ambush and our reinforcement attack. Two HMMWVs arrived behind our rear tank and passed us a tow bar for the middle tank, which was deadlined and immobile at this point. We hooked it up to the second tank. We still had fighting going on so we had to ensure the others still have their machine guns down the alley introducing themselves to the enemy. We rigged the bar to another arriving rescue vehicle and had it towed out of there. Once the vehicles were turned around they drove off. The first tank I told you about is now able to reverse out of the alleyway, it flips a U-turn and drives off, without us! There's 35 of us and all the tanks left us there. We had to bump through street by street doing the 'Mogadishu Mile' (reference to when Delta Force and Rangers had to do the same after their battle). We made our way back to the Tigris River where U.S. Forces had a blocking position set up. While bumping and bounding (leap-frogging in general terms) across alleyways to get out I remember looking ahead and I could see a line of U.S. military vehicles. They are parked all next to each other at the end of this road up against the river. They're only blocks away; I can see people sitting on these vehicles eating and relaxing while I am still exchanging fire with the enemy. I'm wondering what the hell is going on? We finally get to the last building on the street and we are getting shot at by an enemy fighter. We shot an M203 grenade in the window so we could run to the front of the building that faced the river where all of our friendly forces were. We came around this building we see this whole line, 50 plus vehicles, armored, LAVs, all kinds of folks. Some of the Marines hanging out on top of them are yelling at us, 'What are you shooting at?' Let's just say there was some cursing that went on, something to the effect of, 'Hey assholes! On the backside of this building that you're eating lunch at, we're taking fire!' They had no idea, they were like wow, and they duck back down and put their helmets on. I looked around and there were U.S. forces everywhere. Everyone was parked. It looked like the fight was over, like we just called 'END EXERCISE' to a training event. It was highly weird. I remember I was sitting down on a log, I dropped my Kevlar, and I don't smoke, but this civilian guy sits down next to me and offers me a cigarette. I lit it up and burned it down to the end. I looked around and the city was cheering. Cheering and looting of course; however, the vibe in the air was of celebration. The civilian guy says to me, 'You look like you just got done running a marathon.'

"He looked as if they drove into the city and parked there eight hours ago for a nice visit. I was like, 'How long have you been sitting here, what is going on?' He said, 'Oh we are in the looting hours, it's pretty standard, you know after the war is over everyone just runs around looting. They've been doing it for hours now.' So I tell him I just got done with an eight-hour firefight. He says, 'Oh that was you guys? We thought that was celebratory fire.' Celebratory fire? Was he kidding? I basically told him to 'F' off. Then he tells me he's a reporter for CNN and asks my name and if he can get a live audio feed from me to send back to the states. That was the first time my family heard from me, mind I couldn't talk to them, but it was the first time they heard my voice and knew I was alright."

Tim tells me, "Even though you are in a firefight, you remember funny things that happened. At one point I'm leaning against the door of a house while shooting down the alley against several enemy in downtown Baghdad. The door opens and I half fall in and begin room clearing mode. Well there is a family in there that was supposed to be evacuated and the dad has a gun. I don't shoot because he's not pointing it at us. We clear the room and disarm the man. They are all sitting there and one girl, who's in blue jeans, said, 'I am Nadia. You need something you ask Nadia. Are you hungry?' We are looking at each other in disbelief. Nadia spoke English and went to Baghdad University. At this point mind you, we've began eating chickens, or local food we have found since we were lucky if we received or rationed one MRE meal up front of the RCT. We are making fires in bookcases to cook chickens we find or making bread with local supplies houses normally had. There was no food, no re-supply so what you find locally you ate. So we are in the middle of a firefight, I'm using their doorway as cover so I can shoot out of it, and she is in the kitchen cooking us macaroni, which we happily ate, in the middle of a gun fight! She would duck occasionally to avoid the bullets whizzing by through the house, but she kept on cooking. It was pretty funny then and now to us. I kept a log the best as I could during the war and there were key words I would write since we didn't have any time for full-fledged down time. I remember wanting to remember the generosity of this family so I made a note of Nadia so I wouldn't forget."

My One Nightmare

"At one point I'm in Saddam's palace, the next I'm in an alleyway in an ambush. During this particular ambush, picture three tanks as close as they can be stuck, and us just climbing all over them and around them shooting at enemy. One of the houses nearby that we are trying to break into has this 'Mozambique' style shooter on top; he's lifting the rifle above his head and just firing anywhere not even aiming."

(I call it the Afghan style; if you watch the CNN documentary on the fight at Qual-i-jangi fortress at Marzar-e-Sharif on YouTube you will see what I'm talking about.)

"We take down a wall with a grenade and jump over it. I'm taking point, blazing through this house doing CQB . . . there's a point to this story, but there has got to be a reason I was taking point that day, and I soon found out what it was. We were in a big room, we had four guys who were going to go right and a couple of guys were going to go left with me to clear this big 30 x 30 room. The first thing I see going left is this guy in a muscle shirt tucked into nice slacks with his arms straight out to his side (insinuating a hands-up position but they were out straight to his sides). There was another guy who was older, who sheepishly stood there next to him; he looked like his assistant. The guy in the muscle shirt definitely looked like an important person standing up straight and proud. It looked like he was an executive with his assistant. They are standing about 10 feet away from me. I close the distance and I drop him to his knees without lethal force. The corporals do the same with the other unknown in the room. We zip tie them both, finish clearing the room, then drag them outside. They are both standing there flex cuffed and amazed I didn't shoot them and wondering if I was going to now out in the street as they would do to their own people. I point down the road and kick the guy in the muscle shirt in his ass and sent him running. He stumbled a bit but then got his balance and took off in a full sprint. They

47

both took off running. They weren't supposed to be there and the city was supposed to be completely evacuated after notices were delivered of our arrival via our government to avoid civilian casualties. I go back in the house and one of the Corporals on the team is yelling for me to come to the back of the house where there was an alleyway. Well there was an SUV parked there with the back end open. I walk over to the SUV and what do I see hanging there . . . an Iraqi General's uniform. There was a suitcase filled with dinar and another with U.S. one-hundred dollar stacks and a third suitcase of clothes. It hit me; that guy was a General and I just sent him running! I ran back through the house back to the street to see if I can see him. I caught a glimpse of him turning left about 200 yards down the road and there he went, out of sight. Evidently he was getting ready to leave town. To this day, that incident haunts me. It's the only nightmare I have; he is the guy, my guy, who got away. He was one of the guys on the deck of cards. It was gross."

Tim doesn't swear and he laughs a lot; he truly is a gentleman and I had to laugh when interviewing him because I would have been swearing like a sailor during that story but he just refers to it as gross. The deck of cards he mentioned were actual cards created by the US Military identifying the most high ranking and most wanted members of Saddam's government. Tim then tells me for the record, "That was one time I didn't have to crap inside a vehicle because it was on his desk in his house."

You Can't Hesitate When It's Go Time

"After Baghdad we moved up to Tikrit during Operation Tripoli looking for Saddam. We ended up in a battle in Ba'Qubah uncovering large weapon caches. After several more months running foot patrols and hunting the enemy and establishing security in As Samarra and the Al Qadisiyah district we returned to the States."

During that war Tim received a Navy and Marine Corps Commendation Medal with Valor and a Purple Heart Medal for wounds received by the enemy.

"With as many targets as we had, there were far more people (Iraqis) that surprised us who didn't shoot because they didn't have a weapon or there was women and children with them. We don't shoot unless we are being aimed or shot at. We never put ourselves in a position or our chain of command in a position where we had to explain anything . . . except for one time. That incident was televised and documented by ABC *Nightline News*. What ended up happening was I set up a choke point on a street, at 'General's Corner,' during one night when the vehicles were going to refuel just before we were going to go raid an Iraqi Republican Guard barracks which was a Division Objective. About 20 Marines and myself were going to take over the barracks that possibly had a large amount of enemy in there. We set up a choke point in a major intersection to stop incoming traffic. We moved a dump truck to protect us from any vehicles that wanted to race toward us. It was common practice to shoot a tracer round from the choke point if you see a vehicle coming towards you, like a warning signal. We had a vehicle already attempt to run the checkpoint and after fatally engaging the vehicle the driver was identified as an Iraqi Republican Guard General. Usually when the vehicles see the tracer, they stop. Up to this point, only enemy forces had tried to attack the checkpoints. It was simple stuff and it works 99% of the time. This day we encountered the .1% when it didn't work. It's about 2am and I'm in the middle of my pre-combat checks and inspections getting ready to do the raid on the enemy compound. I'm probably about 600 yards from the intersection where we had set up the choke point earlier and I see vehicle headlights driving towards the choke point in the distance. I see the tracer round go off, then I see another tracer go off, and then a third tracer go off. All the while I hear the engine of the vehicle open up and accelerate. Then our machine guns open up in perfect angles of fire to stop the vehicle from running the choke point, attacking, or being a suicide bomber. The vehicle ends up flipping over one of the ABC *Night-line News* reporters and his teammate who is the cameraman; picture the General Lee in the *Dukes of Hazard* sailing through the air, that's what this short bus did. Well when the vehicle came crashing down to a deadly stop, the Marines went over to investigate and they found that the occupants of the vehicle were all women and children with one middle-aged male driver who apparently said screw it, I'm gunning it. Thankfully, ABC reported the grave news in a fair light of the Marines because of the situations we were put in. That incident could have made the news with a different twist that would have had projected U.S. Forces in a really bad way. It was a horrid scene and many Marines who heard the screams from the women and children that night, still hear them today. The Marines at that choke point manning the machine guns were nineteen-year-old young Marines making decisions, but it was the right decision; however it's still a lot of responsibility for a nineteen-year-old."

I asked why the driver ran the gate—and Tim says,

"Stupid is and stupid does. I have no idea. You shake your head wondering what goes through theirs. This wasn't a quick event, he was over 800 yards away from the choke point when the first tracer was shot. At 800, 600, 400 yards the vehicle was warned. At the very limit of an explosion ring we were forced to engage with the machine guns. He went from about forty miles per hour up to about sixty-five-plus miles per hour and gunned it towards the Marines. Stupid decision on his part, right decision on ours, and no ability to decide by his passengers. He was either heading to Baghdad or heading north, maybe trying to get women and children out? We have no idea. There is a reason why machine gunners and Infantry Marines aren't taught to, nor expected to hesitate concerning threats. Hesitation kills. Hesitation will breed delay and the enemy will seize that moment. It's a horrible situation; on many sides, it looks bad for us and then those Marines have to live with their decisions and what they did, even though it was the right thing, they have to live with the aftermath that the driver forced them to face."

I asked if there were any survivors and Tim doesn't think there were but he wasn't sure because he heard the screams from woman and children from inside the van when he was patrolling to his raid on the compound. Even though they had a mission, I tell him I don't blame him for wanting to get off that target in an instant.

He says, "Ya, that screaming stays with you."

I can't imagine how the nineteen-year-old machine gunners felt that night, for doing their job. Tim told me what happened after was just as horrific. The young Marines had to pull all the bodies from the van and they buried them, thinking it was the right thing to do by giving them a proper burial. The next morning the unit makes them dig up the bodies to turn them over to local authorities for a proper burial. So not only do they have to hear the screaming of the women and children as they are laying down fire on the van running the checkpoint, but they have to see the dead bodies of the women and children they just killed the night prior again, after being in the ground for the night.

"That had to be the worst decision a command ever made, having the same guys who killed them dig them up. They should not see the humanity of their actions while still being asked to implement their skill set. They are professionals to the T and to instill doubt is not conducive to preserving life."

PRIORITIES: I GOT TO DO MY THING, AND I'M GONNA DO IT AGAIN

It's the end of 2003, beginning of 2004, Tim finally returns safely home and gets to meet his daughter for the first time; she was four months old. He tells me trying to integrate back into family life was interesting. His priority was to go off to war, and he got to do his thing, now his priority is to get to know his family, and maybe get out of the Marine Corps.

"It was somewhat quiet in Iraq during the first few months until the beginning of 2004 when things starting ramping up again. 2/4 took over the Ramadi mission in Al Anbar Province. They had a tough deployment as a Battalion and they were taking mass casualties." Tim says, "Perhaps it was because 2/4 was in Okinawa throughout the war and they weren't in combat. They never worked through their bugs like we all did in 2003. They got extended in Okinawa for six more months so they were there for a year when the war finished up. They came back to the states and then deployed to the most dangerous city there was, Ramadi. 2/4 was getting a lot of enemy sniper activity."

Back stateside, Tim took over the Scout Sniper Platoon once Brent Clearman departed (RIP) and was asked to go assist and deploy again. He talked to his wife and told her he was going to stay on for one more deployment. He had about 11 more months at home before he had to head out again back to Iraq. He began training his guys in some unconventional ways.

Being in FAST Company taught him a lot of skills he passed on to his team:

"Urban sniping, urban patrolling, not just the rural stalks. For example Camp Pendleton has a camp on it called Camp Telega. It's the farthest point north on Camp Pendleton where *Heartbreak Ridge* was filmed. Beyond Camp Telega is Orange County, California. There is a field, or valley, then a ridge lined with houses in Orange County. Up on this ridge was an animal shelter. So I'm trying to think of new ways to train my guys in urban warfare and I have this idea about using the animal shelter. I ask the shelter if I can park a pickup truck up there to observe and spot my guys trying to sneak over to the shelter. I explained it was training and I had spoken to the sheriff's department to clear it. They were fine with it. I sent my guys out on patrols and they would have to do stalks to the objective, which was my pickup truck in the parking lot of the animal shelter. They were to get within 200 yards of the objective and log in all activity in the vicinity. What I didn't tell the guys was that there were volunteers constantly outside walking dogs on and off paths and playing Frisbee—some obstacles to make their training a little harder. So they had to try different things to get around their scent being picked up by the dogs and not get compromised. I also trained them to move around malls and talk to each other without being next to each other. Being in mass personnel areas with a high flow of people would come into play during some street patrols or market area patrols later. We had lock picking classes, etc. Other Battalions started to get wind of what I was training my Battalion in and so 3/5 sent me their entire Sniper element to train. I ran Indocs and started screening guys for them so we could combine the sniper elements into one Indoc—which hadn't happened in a long time. We trained them very well. We were determined to have the best trained platoon there could be. I was getting reports back as to what was happening with 2/4 in Iraq and I was telling my Battalion Commander the techniques I would incorporate when over there. I wanted him to know we wouldn't just be sitting on our post, we would be unconventional. We would be more aggressive and proactive with locations we would use. The 2/4 Sniper Platoons were getting backfilled with infantry guys in country since Scout Snipers are a limited resource (approx. 220 in the entire Marine Corps at that time). 2/4 had a Scout Sniper team with one Sniper and 3 infantry Marines who were killed while on post.

"After the team was killed, the enemy took the M40 sniper rifle off of the fallen Marine. We now have the enemy running around with one of our rifles which will be used against us. It was our job, my job, to get it back and kill whoever took it. I failed in that mission but am proud as hell of 3/5 for not failing."

So, with his wife's consent, Tim is back in Iraq. Within the first week of being back in country, in Ramadi, the weapons company commander in charge of the area for Tim's Platoon said it was too much for him and he resigned his commission on the spot. This is highly unique and unheard of.

"He's the unicorn; you never hear of that. Complete abandonment of his men. The Battalion Commander puts his Assistant Operations Officer in charge and within a week he gets killed. ABC *Nightline* again is following them and they chose to follow the Captain who they had to tell the nation again of another lost Marine as they did for the First Sergeant on the last deployment. I went to the Battalion Commander and said 'Sir, the chains have to come off.' The enemy knows exactly what we can see from our positions, and we can work around that. I told him what I would be doing and I would report to him and he said very well. It felt from that night on, we went out as Scout Snipers conducting mission after mission only to come back to refit with ammo and reequip. The enemy went from being confident with the upper hand to dumbfounded and confused at where to fear the eye in the sky they couldn't hide from. When we started incorporating our new TTPs [tactics, techniques and procedures], I knew the enemy didn't have a clue as to what we were doing. We started engaging them from undisclosed locations; not where they figured we would be even if covered and concealed. They had no idea where we were. This was the time we were seeing Wanted posters up of us. Intelligence began reporting that the enemy communication began targeting us and putting out awards or bounties for Marines with scoped rifles. We had bounties on our heads and we knew it meant we were doing well but it would also affect the Snipers to deploy into the area after us such as Chris Kyle. We had to continue to get stealthier. We no longer did the typical HMMWV ride up to a building, enter en masse, and post watch up on the roof. The stuff we were doing went above and beyond. We were breaking into houses, picking locks or quietly breaking locks. We were using all sorts of skills taught in Sniper School Basic Course and many others that were taught from a wide variety of expertise inside and out of the Marine Corps.

"We would sit about seven blocks back from our objective with a visual tunnel on whatever we wanted to watch then we would break into the house after watching it, tie up the entire family, and when we left we left them tied up! I don't care how they get out but I am not letting them go so they could spread the word that we are in the area so we can get killed. And I'm not breaking any rules by keeping them tied; I'm just extending our lives. I could give a shit how they get out after we left, I'm not letting them go so they can rat on us and we get killed. More likely the next morning they got up and ran out. While we were in a house that we took over, we would make the women do their regular activities like making bread in the morning or whatever as to not draw attention to the fact we were in the house and shooting out of it. It was a target rich environment. My goal was to make sure our Battalion Commander didn't have to answer for any of our shots that we took."

TAKE THE REPORTER INSIDE THE BUILDING

"One incident got a little too close for comfort that could have caused the Colonel concern. We had been in this house for a day and half and I've already laid out the distances to the intersection outside, to the buildings nearby with dark shadows that I can't see into. I assessed the area and knew it pretty good. So as we're sitting on a roof looking down the road we see this guy on a moped with a guy on the back circling the intersection I told you about. There was a hole in the ground in the middle of a roundabout in the intersection. Sure enough 'Moped Joe' comes around, circles the hole twice, drops the guy off on the back who has a pack, and then the guy tries to drop the bag in the hole and then I drop the guy with the bag. The guy on the moped takes off. One of the other Sniper Teams in that building with me, 'Shadow 4,' takes a shot at the guy on the moped but doesn't get the hit, and he disappears down the alleyway and he's gone. About 10 minutes later 'Moped Joe' comes back again, with another passenger on the back, circles the hole, and drops this guy off near the hole. As he goes to drag the bag to the hole, because the bag is just lying there on the ground still, Shadow 4 drops him. This scenario goes on for another 40 minutes with each of us taking turns at shooting. The COC (Command Operations Center, pronounced as "see-o-see") and I talk via radio. The Watch Officer tells me I never have to call in for permission for anything; I just have to do my job and report it afterwards, which I already knew. I had called in the two previous kills, 'Be advised Shadow 8 engaged, Shadow 4 engaged a guy on a moped dropping off passengers with a bag they are trying to conceal in a hole, etc.' 'Roger.' Again, 'Be advised moped guy is back, Shadow 8 engaged second passenger trying to put the bag in a hole.' So then I call up and say, 'Shadow 8 requesting permission to continue to engage targets from moped.' The reply back was, 'Shadow 8, you've never called in permission before, just stay up there and do your job. Are you alright? What's wrong?' I reply back, 'Well, I just want absolute permission to engage these targets when the age group of his passengers has gone down in the last 40 minutes from 25-year-old males to now boys the age of my daughter (younger than 12).' COC gives the 'cease fire' and said they would send in armored HMMWVS to try to deter the situation. So some of the mental aspects of what we do while deployed tie back to your home life. I know you have to give 100% attention to the mission, no matter what it is, to be successful. You have to compartmentalize. I would come back from the mission, send an email to the wife, once a week at best for 10 minutes we would talk on the satellite phone, but that's it, other than that it was 100% live eat breath my weapon, my next insert point.

"When you're sitting out there, and *American Sniper* covered it, you have some hefty decisions to make that weigh on your conscience. One time we were patrolling with a Company of Infantry Marines, about 100 to 200 guys. We were doing a sweep through the city and we end up taking machine gun fire and we all scrambled into different buildings. My Snipers and I along with an AP reporter jump into a house. Shadow 4 and myself are up on the rooftop. A couple guys are inside the house to make sure nobody bombarded it. It was a two-story house at the end of a long T-shaped road. So we are at the 'T' looking down this long road taking heavy machine gun fire from about 400 yards down the road from both left and right sides lighting up our building.

"The Associated Press (AP) reporter is on the rooftop with us lying in a fetal position, crying with his camera sideways, snapping pictures saying, 'I hate my job! I hate my job!' Meanwhile the Infantry Marines in other buildings were dealing with their own firefights from surrounding enemy. We were trying to punch holes in the brick wall so we could get a visual and try to engage the enemy. Then we start taking heavy fire on both sides of the building. We're all crouching down and running around as low as possible. Two other Marine Snipers with us are taking shots; they later were killed on another mission that deployment, God rest their souls. We try to put the 50 caliber SASR to work because we can see where they are shooting from but we can't see them. They are shooting from these hacienda-style courtyards and engaging us heavily. We are trying to shoot through the courtyard steel doors, no luck. About 5 to 10 minutes into the firefight one side of the street stops firing. We don't know what's going on. Then we see this little girl walk over from the quiet side to the active side. She goes in the building and comes back out minutes later with a belt of ammunition to resupply the quiet side! They send her over twice across the street to get more ammunition and at some point we had to say, we have to stop the source of this problem. The Team Leader and myself know what needs to happen. The other guys are on their rifles. Who can live with that for the rest of their lives?"

Tim had a little girl at home. If he did it, would he be reminded of it every time he looks at his little girl? This is what snipers have to live with. We all have tough decisions to make in life but I don't think many can compare to the decision Tim and his Team Leader were faced with that day. So the enemy sends the girl over for the third time. Shadow 4 section leader and Tim were forced to make the decision.

"That's why we get paid to make the big decisions. We're pinned down, we have an AP reporter with us, whether you shoot the girl or you don't shoot the girl there is a very bad story that is going to come out of this for the girl or for our families. Shadow 4 section leader and myself decided to have him take the AP reporter into the house. Then the machine guns were silent. Some of those decisions that your training has prepared you to make still sit with you, when they shouldn't because you know it was the right decision, but they still never leave the mind. You know that the people you are fighting beside and the people back home in my country want me to do this, and I understand the politics and agendas of people but what people don't understand is what our (snipers) agenda is. People will tell us that it's to kill but as a Christian kid who grew up with morals my agenda was to stop the genocide, stop the people who are causing the genocide. If that means to stand up and take action then so be it. When you look at Ramadi on Google Earth and zoom in and you can see that a third of the city is a graveyard/body dump. They would just dump the bodies of people who didn't want to conform. People who they shot in the head, women they raped, they threw them all in there. The bodies numbered thousands so who would I be as a man not to take action against that and stop it? I have 'engaged and neutralized' many targets, but I have kicked soccer balls around and shook hands with a thousand more Iraqis than those that I have ended. And the ones I have killed are trying to kill us, and killing innocent people. People don't understand that. If someone wants to shoot at me I'm going to shoot back and protect my life. Some say but 'you are in their country,' yes, but I'm trying to save the majority of that country's people from the genocide I can see happening in front of my own eyes. I have patrolled through that graveyard, 10 guys walking at midnight through this 10 to 15 click [a click is a kilometer] graveyard to the south of Ramadi so we could watch the city from the darkness, that was haunting. And we'd catch locals sneaking out there at night! There's people in the USA illegally but I don't go around shooting at them, like I shouldn't be shot at for just being in Iraq, does that make sense? Back home doesn't always understand this, they haven't seen or smelled the bodies, heard the screams, or understand the mass killings of the Kurds to the North. Ramadi was the wild, wild West. It was full on engagement 100% of the time."

Jared Had the Last Laugh, God Bless Him and his Family

"I was crossing a dark alleyway over a median on an ambient lit street into another dark alleyway making our way to a house. It was typical fashion for the one or two guys on point to peer out from the darkness to look at the length of the street in the direction we are going to move to, bound across the street [like leap-frogging], then the next two go and so on. On this particular night, the first two Marines looked left and right, bounded about twenty yards across the street and into the next alley facing forward. The next group of guys to go include me. As we go across the street someone detonates an IED daisy chain. This IED was meant to take out armored vehicles and we were on foot. I sailed across the street from the blast and landed at the entrance to the next alleyway. I immediately get up and start scurrying over to the middle of the street to regroup on the safe side. I come across Shadow 4, and he has a huge hole in his chest. He's gone. I can see another marine lying in the street nearby motionless, and I run over and start stripping him down checking his vitals and looking for wounds to no avail. Checking his groin and armpit for artery bleeding. I can't find any bleeding. So I start chest compressions. He had been dipping at the time he died so I go to do mouth to mouth and get a mouthful of his dip. God bless him, I love him. I cleared his passageway and start doing chest compressions. Both marines were about two feet on either side of me and they both died instantly from that IED; somehow I got launched about 20 feet. I had severe leg injuries and shrapnel everywhere, but somehow I lived. The two guys on point still in the alleyway both lived but they each took about 8–10 holes in their backs and one of the guys' arms was shattered. On the friendly side of the alley the next Marine to bump across holding security took facial shrapnel. We ended up dragging the two bodies off the street into a compound yard area. We are all in a circle around each other performing first aid on everyone.

"While I was still trying to resuscitate the first marine another was putting tourniquets on my legs. I'm doing chest compressions with a pistol in my hand; another marine is trying to get a radio functioning after it was damaged. We're collecting weapons because at that point I'm thinking one, we are going to get a counter attack and two, we are still looking for a stolen Scout Sniper rifle that the enemy has and there are more out in the street. We destroyed the stuff we couldn't carry and from there . . ."

(At this point in the story Tim lets out this sigh, and stumbles for words. He's an upbeat guy but I heard the anguish in his voice as he recalled this story. Even though it was a phone interview, I can hear Tim when he smiles as he talks; he was not smiling now. What I heard created a mental picture of him contorting his face in disbelief, and he continues on.)

". . . it sucked a little because it took 45 minutes . . . what ended up happening was, well the story is . . . since we got blown up the raid force was to take down this particular house if anything happened to us so they launched a medevac team with that raid force. We were inserting to do pre-raid surveillance for a high value target, Abu Musab al-Zarqawi (mentioned in *American Sniper*). The eight of us waited about 45 minutes, bleeding out, and finally two HMMWVs find us and we load up one HMMWV with the two dead Marines, the two pointmen that were wounded severely along with all the gear, and the remaining Marines beside myself and one other since there wasn't any more room by any means. My pants were basically blown off and I could fit a beer bottle through the hole in my leg. The one HMMWV drives away so me and another Marine are waiting to get in the other HMMWV. Well it drives up to us and then by us following the first one! We are sitting there stranded. So I had to convince the homeowner of where we were at to give us his car by showing my pistol and a $20 (we kept money on us in case we had to bribe someone—for instances just like this) and I said 'car keys.' He spoke English and gave me his car keys. All I could think was that some Lance Corporal on post is gonna wax me when I try to enter base, but I'm gonna give it a try anyway. I need to get us back to the base on the west side of Ramadi. So I tape big 'Xs' on the hood of this Iraqi's car with duct tape, I put my IR beacon on the antenna, and I put IR Chem lights on the windshield wipers. So we borrowed his car and medevac'd ourselves back to camp."

Tim made it back to camp and he made it back home, as you will read.

PTSD Is Not a Disorder; It's Just another Reality

"As a Sniper you are given the trust and confidence and the ability to be judge and jury and executioner. You have all these responsibilities and then you get hurt, and all that responsibility is over. I got hit by that IED on November 4th. I called my wife right away, like I had sworn to always do after that first time being wounded. I went through surgery upon surgery in Baghdad. I was home at my house on November 9th. There was no Wounded Warrior Regiment in place back then. There wasn't appropriate accountability and for some no medical care coming back when you returned to the states unless you had a full amputation and were hospitalized (or should have been like I was but was not). I woke up at my house in my own bed. The last conscious memory I had was being in a hospital in Walter Reed. I had remained unconscious on all flights while the flight nurse administered morphine. I had zero hospital care for 6 months. So picture going from the battlefield in that chaotic environment and then you wake up home in your bed. My daughter who was five years old at the time was preparing gauze with saline solution for me, my wife was cleaning out and packing the rotting flesh wound I had in my leg three times a day.

"A volunteer fireman luckily helped us out along with out of state family and also the newly started Injured Marine Semper Fi Fund. I lived on base in base housing. My wife would drive over to medical to pick up the supplies I needed. Week after week she told them I was still bleeding, and all they did was give her a grocery bag with more gauze, saline solution, and pain killers; they wouldn't come over to the house to check on me. There was no tracking, the hospital was full, I was like a ghost, and they didn't know who I was, when or where I got wounded, so 'we' took care of me. After five months the smell of my rotting flesh consumed the house. I lost all the muscle in my leg as the adductor muscles rotted. As I sat there I thought, a minute ago I was king shit with all of this responsibility for the Marine Corps and now, I'm left immobilized with a rotting flesh wound and they won't even take care of me. I was forgotten. It happened to so many guys. Wounded Warrior Regiment is assigned to track down these guys, guys like me, and find them to make sure they get the proper care they deserve. I was supposed to go to the hospital at Naval Hospital on Camp Pendleton or Balboa but I got lost."

Tim tells me he most likely has some PTSD (post-traumatic stress disorder).

"I hate the term PTSD. It's not a 'disorder' it's a reality, it's a different reality, a post-traumatic reality. Look what we go through and then we abruptly wake up back home and are expected to assimilate just fine. You know you would think after the World Wars, Korea, Vietnam the government would have had a plan for the wounded guys when they come home from OEF and OIF. There's abandonment issues, anxiety issues, etc. I ended up going to the hospital in town after six months being home and got skin grafts and got taken care of. I spent 18 months of living on base, no shaving, no haircuts, no working."

He must have felt like he was losing his identity.

"Then the Marine Corps tells me they are just going to medically retire me. Well, I want to stay in; I want to work. So then they started giving us wounded Marines the opportunity to stay in. I enjoy being a Marine first and foremost, I enjoy being a Scout Sniper. So many people ask me, What's your best shot?"

Tim was surprised when I never asked, nor cared to ask, what his best shot or furthest shot was. That is not the point of this story. He tells me he's been asked before though, like it was the most important thing to being a Sniper, and he says:

"I tell people my best shot is at twenty-five yards. At that point you'd damn well have a tight plan on how you are going to defend your position, escape your position, and how you are going to kill everyone in the process because people are coming at you and you better be ready. At 500–1,000+ yards you are lying in prone, you are breathing, you're calm, it's peaceful, and you are applying your fundamentals. I tell people, it's not about killing, it's about living actually. It's about watching our convoys go up and down the streets safely, it's about soldiers coming back and being able to sit with those guys at the chow hall because you just knocked off the dude that was going to slip an IED in a hole in the middle of a traffic circle; it's about the guys who live. It's not about being the crazies going into churches or schools shooting up a bunch of people, it's about being the guy who shoots these people before they conduct mass murders. I can break bread with my friends, with my brothers, and see a movie or attend a congregation and not have to worry about a crazy person to mow us down with gunfire because there's someone watching for him, there's someone in the hide waiting to eliminate him so the rest of us can go about living safely in peace."

CHAPTER FOUR

Target Practice: 1918

O. O. Ellis and E. B. Garey

THE MOST THRILLING EXPERIENCE YOU WILL HAVE AT A TRAINING CAMP will probably come when you step up to the firing line on the target range to fire your first shot. The great majority of new men grow pale, become nervous, lose their calm and poise, while they are on the firing line. This is a fact, not a theory. And this loss of nerve is not confined to the new man. Any shot, however old and experienced, will tell you that he fully understands what we have just described.

To become a good shot, we must solve a mental condition that corresponds in a way to that of beginners in golf. And we must master some details in technique.

We should know something about the machine (rifle) we are to operate. We must know what the sights are and how to use them. We should know how those men most successful in the science and art of shooting hold the rifle under different conditions, how they adjust their slings, how they prepare (blacken) their sights and care for their rifles, what practice and preparation they take, and what bits of advice they have to offer.

The primitive man had no means of accurately aiming his crude devices to throw stones. But in this day and age we have. The modern rifle is one of the most perfect pieces of scientific machinery in the world. Very shortly after you arrive in camp your captain will explain to you its sights and how they are adjusted. The rifle has a sighting bar for that purpose. It will take you only a few minutes to grasp the subject when you have a rifle in your hands, and your instructor is pointing out and explaining just what you should know. On paper it seems to be hard.

Now you will want to learn how to load your piece (rifle), work your bolt, and squeeze the trigger. Simple as these points may seem, you will have something to learn after you have been at it ten years. Practice! practice! practice! Sit on your bunk and work your bolt ten thousand times before you go on the range. Get in the habit of doing it quickly. Learn to keep your piece at your shoulder while you pull the bolt back and push it home. Learn to make the fewest possible motions of your body in working it. To pull a bolt back and push it forward seems to be a simple thing to do. It is simple. But when you are actually firing at the target, experience tells you that you will have more trouble and a greater collection of hard luck stories to amuse your friends with than you ever imagined possible, unless you have had plenty of practice.

To squeeze a trigger seems to be a simple thing to do. It is simple. But after you have been squeezing triggers for twenty years you will have something more to learn about it. Ninety-five percent of the failures on the target range in the training camps come from not squeezing the trigger properly. You can't learn how to squeeze it on paper. You have got to practice. Every time you work your bolt, squeeze your trigger. Get in some extra "squeezes." You will find that your whole muscular and nervous system will need to be coordinated and harmonized. After you have been long about it you will find an extreme delicacy in its operation. You will find that it requires a great deal more than a finger. All the muscles of your hand and arm will be required. We cannot overemphasize the importance of squeezing your trigger. When you learn to do this without jumping (flinching), without moving an eyelash, you are making progress and are prepared for more advanced work.

Why do you suppose we have "gallery practice," that is, practice with a greatly reduced charge of powder? Simply to determine and correct your errors. We assume that you have normal sight and that you are in fair physical condition. Suppose that you make a perfect score. What conditions must you fulfill?

First, you must aim in exactly the same way every time.

Second, at the instant of firing your body must be in perfect repose.

Third, you must squeeze your trigger properly (without a jerk).

You could not aim exactly the same way every time unless you understood your sights and unless you could see them plainly. You will be told to blacken them. Many forget and fail to do this. They do not fully realize that the sights are much easier to see when blackened, and that therefore the chances of hitting the bull's-eye are much greater. There's no more luck in shooting than there is in solving a problem in geometry, or in a game of billiards. It's all practice, nerve, and science.

Your body cannot be in repose at the instant you fire unless you have your sling properly adjusted, unless you are reasonably comfortable (not constrained), and unless you, temporarily, stop breathing. Your body must be, for an instant, a vise. Any trivial thing such as a puff of wind, a jerk of the trigger, or a noise near you, will ordinarily change your hold and throw you off the bull's-eye.

Suppose you are making a poor score. What is the trouble? In the first place don't blame it on the rifle or the ammunition. Assume full responsibility yourself. You are the responsible party. Practice a great deal and see if you can locate the fault. If you cannot, your captain will assist you.

When we go from gallery practice to the target range, where we fire the service rifle with the service charge, we find a great difference in the recoil of the rifle and in the sound. The good Lord has made our muscles and nervous system to react automatically at danger or anything connected with it. That is probably why we shudder and close our eyes when a door is slammed very near to us. But sound, unless we get too close, does not hurt anyone, and we should steel our nerves to remember that fact when we are firing. We also know that there is going to be a certain amount of recoil of the rifle. But if you will hold your sling as you have been instructed, if you will provide yourself with proper elbow and shoulder padding, the authors of this text assure you that you will experience no pain or harm from the recoil. It is their judgment that if you are healthy and can see and will go on the range with your jaws set to fire with anything like your gallery practice coolness, and calmness, you will qualify. Your greatest stumbling block will be your rapid fire. This is where you fire a definite number of shots in a limited time. And this is where you will experience the extreme amount of nervousness.

When you return from firing your first score at rapid fire, and have had time to think calmly over your actions, you will probably realize that your nerves were pitched up and that you did a number of foolish things. You should realize that you are not an exceptional man. Ninety-nine out of every hundred normal, virile men are more or less nervous when they first step up for rapid fire. Practice and will power are the correctives.

Let us suppose that you have ten shots to fire in two minutes. If you fire your ten shots in one minute it is plain that you return unused one minute given to you. This minute may have been of great use to you in getting closer to the bull's-eye. If you fire at the rate of ten shots in three minutes, it is plain that when your two minutes shall have expired you have missed the opportunity of firing four times at the bull's-eye.

Get one of your bunkies to go back of your tent and time you. Then swap about and you hold the watch for him. Try to make of yourself a machine that finishes the ten shots just before the time expires.

And here is a little rule of thumb we want you to bear constantly in mind while you are having rapid fire: Load your piece quickly, but aim and squeeze your trigger deliberately. Keep cool.

The best shot in the company is the man who practices the most.

CHAPTER FIVE

The Hide Site: Three Stories

Gina Cavallaro and Matt Larsen

WHEN THE FIRST GULF WAR BEGAN, THERE WERE MANY UNITS WHOSE mission was what Special Forces soldiers called "special reconnaissance."

These included certain Special Forces A-teams as well as Army long-range reconnaissance and surveillance, or LRRS, units and Marine Force Reconnaissance teams.

Special reconnaissance meant infiltrating deep into enemy territory according to an established doctrine that dictated up to a certain number of kilometers, and pulling surveillance, or putting "eyes on," an important terrain feature such as a road intersection or a main supply route.

The idea behind special reconnaissance was to establish a secret observation post, or hide site, close enough to the terrain feature or other objective to be able to observe it but far enough away that no one on it would ever expect you to be there and catch or compromise you.

This doctrine had been developed over the years since World War II with the assumption that we'd be fighting the large conventional armies of that era. In Europe, for instance, the LRRS units planned to go to ground and let the Soviet juggernaut roll over them before establishing their surveillance positions in the enemy's rear.

Unrealized was the fact that this doctrine presupposed a disinterested populace. This was, after all, doctrine written by an army that had known almost twenty years of peace following the withdrawal of the major units from Vietnam.

The last time U.S. forces had fought in large numbers in a foreign desert was during World War II when we battled against German and Italian forces in a region populated by North Africans who had no dog in the fight, so to speak. The doctrine was to be tested soon after the air war commenced in the Gulf War in 1991.

In August 1990 the U.S. began the movement of a half-million troops to Saudi Arabia where they staged along the border with Iraq in response to Saddam Hussein's invasion of Kuwait.

As part of that action, various American and coalition Special Operations units were given the task of searching across Iraq for Scud missile launchers, which were showering their deadly payload on civilian neighborhoods in Saudi Arabian and Israeli cities.

One of these units was the storied British Special Air Service, or SAS. The plan for its initial insertion was to fly hundreds of miles into the Iraqi rear and establish surveillance on the main roads exiting the Baghdad area.

On the first night of the mission, several teams were to infiltrate by helicopter and then continue their infiltration by foot and establish hide sites overlooking the main and secondary travel routes. When the first team got into the area of its planned infil, it flew over the terrain and realized that it wasn't going to work. Even from inside the helicopter, the team members could tell that the barren landscape offered little chance of remaining hidden. The second team landed but it called for its helicopter to return almost as soon as the bird flew away. It also determined that the chances of success were small.

Only one team that night continued on with the plan. That eight-man team, which would be known to history by its radio call sign Bravo Two Zero, was compromised by a little boy herding goats on the first morning of the mission. The men on that ill-fated team were forced to evade capture and try to escape more than two hundred miles to the border with Turkey. But it was futile. All save one were killed or captured in the attempt.

The doctrine that dictated the planning and execution of that mission was flawed partly in assuming the terrain would be more forgiving. But the more colossal oversight was the failure to take into account the people of the region and the way they live.

The little goatherd understood that those foreign men weren't there to fight other foreign men as was the case in North Africa during World War II. He and his family understood that they were there to fight Iraqi soldiers, at the very least, or them.

For people raised in the United States or Western Europe, it is easy to imagine remaining concealed while very close to civilization, partly because these areas don't have nor do they tolerate nomadic tribes. Few people in these regions make their homes outside the offerings of a robust infrastructure and, at least in America, walking to and from anything, except in a major city, simply put, is rare.

Most Americans leave their homes by getting directly into their cars and driving to the parking lot where they are headed. Even children stay inside more and more and watch television or play video games rather than roam the countryside playing.

In the Middle East and Southwestern Asia, this is not the case. People in these regions live on the land, walking distances wildly unimaginable elsewhere.

Today's sniper teams in search of a hide site can probably count on someone like the goatherd who compromised Bravo Two Zero walking in on them eventually, even in what seems to be the most remote reaches of desert.

In Afghanistan's natural environment, Special Forces sniper teams perform a combination of missions, from over-watches of people and villages to direct assaults to providing covering fire for a force package. Watching the approach of a goatherd and gauging his intent is part of the job and the risk. Getting compromised happens all the time.

"Just when you think you're not on a goat trail, the goat herder happens upon you. He sees you, you flex-cuff him, and you leave. Somebody finds him a few hours later. He says, 'The Americans were here, they flex-cuffed me, and they left.' You're a fool if you stay in that area," said Sgt. First Class Joey of the Third Special Forces Group.

Another aspect of society in America and Western Europe is the prevalence of a multiethnic society. It's easy to blend in, especially in larger cities, regardless of ethnicity. As was the case in Vietnam, the fairly homogeneous societies of Iraq and Afghanistan make American and coalition soldiers stand out like redheaded babies in a Chinese maternity ward.

The Green Berets have learned plenty of tricks to staying concealed during their thousands of missions in the mountains, hills, and wadis of Afghanistan.

One is dressing for success. They have worn and continue to wear a mixture of clothes, and they never, ever wear the Army's digital camouflage pattern, known as the universal camouflage pattern. The ineffectiveness of the pattern, which was fielded in 2005, for the variety of terrains in Afghanistan was recognized early on by Special Forces troops.

Among the items they've worn is the popular Multicam pattern, which was even authorized almost begrudgingly by the regular Army in 2010 for all soldiers headed to Afghanistan.

"Early in the war we wore a mix of civilian clothing and local garb like blue jeans or man jammies or whatever the locals were wearing. We all had beards back then and didn't cut our hair for a while so we were shaggy as we could get," Sgt. First Class Joey said. Still, he said, the locals always knew they didn't belong because the villages are tight—they all know each other, and they can spot an outsider from more than a mile away.

This challenge carries over to urban operations in Iraq as well.

"If you drive a car into a neighborhood in Iraq, everybody in that neighborhood knows every car. So you may get away with it once, but you're definitely not going to get away with it twice. On a second pass to get a photo or something, somebody's going to know," he said.

By the same token, if villagers in Afghanistan see an outsider milling around a mountainside where there is usually no one, they're more than likely going to check it out and they'll do it with guns in hand.

Protective equipment is optional in some cases, and for the unforgiving, vertical terrain in Afghanistan, it can even be a disadvantage. Soldiers deploying to Afghanistan began wearing the lighter plate carriers when it was acknowledged, after years of fighting that often took place on the face of a steep hill, that the heavier gear bogged down a soldier, inhibiting his speed and agility. The gear also created an untold number of musculoskeletal injuries.

Special Forces soldiers, who work in small teams and have more flexibility in what they wear, shoot, and carry, opted for the lighter gear years before the conventional Army did.

"In a city, you better have body armor on, but in Afghanistan, there's been times we've been without body armor because at 11,000 feet, if you think you're going to climb a mountain with body armor on and be worth a darn when you get to the top or if you think you're going to chase some half-naked Taliban guy down a foot trail with body armor on at that kind of elevation, you're mistaken," said Sgt. First Class Ricky of the Third Special Forces Group.

That kind of flexibility for Special Forces soldiers, whose missions are stacked toward the snatch-and-grab variety versus the intersection over-watch type, was critical when it came to time-sensitive missions, which happened more often than the long-lasting hide and wait missions.

"These targets don't stay in one place for a very long time. The reality of dropping a sniper team kilometers away out of earshot of a helicopter and having them walk through that type of terrain and over-watch that target, if you want to really catch the guy, is not always realistic," Sgt. First Class Ricky said, pointing out that a long infiltration also has logistical concerns with provisions, depending on the length of stay. "The two-man sniper team crawling on their belly up to take a shot on a guy is, I'm not going to say unrealistic, it's not the norm these days."

GUTS, GUNS, AND GARBAGE

Cities get smaller and smaller when you're a sniper in need of a loophole. The more hide sites you find and use, the fewer there are for new missions. And it's especially hard when you stand out to begin with.

With the exception of a few who have certain physical traits, American infantrymen walk, talk, look, and smell like Americans. Not to mention the American uniform, an instant identifier the enemy has no obligation to wear.

When Sgt. Derek Balboa was faced with finding a hide site for an over-watch mission on the outskirts of Mosul, a city of nearly two million people in northern Iraq, he and his partner went to the most unpleasant, outside-the-box idea they knew of.

It was a disgusting way to carry out a mission, but the wet, rotting, offal-laden garbage dump—in which they spent three days lying on their bellies—ended up being the crown jewel of hide sites, the king daddy of concealment.

Okay. It should be mentioned that they did get compromised by a peripatetic goatherd, but Balboa said he still considered the mission a success because the reconnaissance, planning, and execution of the dump-as-hide-site concept was proven.

"All that together tells me that the idea would work," said Balboa, an affable young patriot from Illinois who quit his job as a construction worker and joined the Army on the spot when he saw the television images of New York's twin towers crumbling to the ground on 9/11.

When he decided to serve his country, he hadn't envisioned the part with the stinking trash pit, but the day he and his partner came up with the idea—"we'd heard about some Marines or a British team doing it"— they enthusiastically started outlining their plan.

The mission itself, to over-watch a surveillance camera, had become an occasional standard with Balboa's leaders, a method of baiting criminals into the sights of their snipers by placing a real, or sometimes bogus, camera on a utility pole or some other high spot and waiting for someone to come along and shoot at it. And they almost always did, even though it was announced to the public that there were snipers in the area who were authorized to kill those who tried to disable the cameras.

"Messages had already gone out in the media that if anyone was caught messing with the cameras, it would be necessary for us to use lethal force. Other sniper and recon teams were engaging guys who did this so they knew there were going to be consequences," said Balboa, who noted that the knowledge that snipers were watching an area generally had a calming effect on the enemy.

"It demoralizes the insurgency because they know you're out there, and nobody wants to move; your stomach's going to be clenched just walking around. Even if there wasn't much going on and we weren't catching them, we were still denying them freedom of movement on the battlefield. I didn't like the fact that they knew I was there, but just by my sheer presence we might have saved someone's life."

The realistic-looking decoy cameras were usually made with ammunition cans painted black with some kind of cylindrical "lens" and were then affixed to a visible point overhead. The baiting idea was hatched when the battalion's intelligence section kept reporting that other surveillance cameras they installed at known areas of trouble were being regularly shot and disabled.

A camera was posted alluringly on the southwest end of town in a poverty-stricken area, a corner of Mosul with a mix of tumbledown tenements and crumbling abandoned buildings that overlooked a vast garbage dump from about four hundred meters away.

In Iraq, many garbage dumps are simply empty lots or fields that are covered with various layers of waste and refuse and sometimes, especially in an urban area, abut neighborhoods. The people who live there walk into the field and dump their garbage.

It was perfect, almost too perfect.

The recon a couple of days before they set in was done in broad daylight, and the sniper team got a good look at—and a good whiff of—the squalid place it was thinking of calling home for three days. The gritty reality of the plan sank in like the *Titanic*.

"These buildings were horrible; there was just nothing. I looked at my buddy, and we started looking out in the trash and we're like, 'I don't know, man.' We're both thinking the same thing. I was like, 'I do not want to be sitting in this,' but the commander was all over it. We're like, 'Sure, because you don't have to sit in it.'"

Beyond the dump to the south was a hardscrabble wasteland that disappeared into open desert. They could infiltrate from there.

In the dump itself, the sniper team saw the same thing at the same time—a section with two piles of trash and an open area with a backstop, a dip that looked directly toward the target they wanted to watch. The closest buildings were a good five hundred meters away and were on a slight hill. The chances of being seen because something looked out of place, they thought, were slim.

"Most people in the country don't have jobs. They know what their neighborhood looks like, and they're pretty much clued in to their habitat. But they're not clued in to their trash," Balboa said, pointing out that the landscape in the dump changed with the wind and the rummaging of goats, "so we could move stuff around and it wouldn't matter."

They took pictures as they drove away and went back to their planning table to nail down the details.

"Everybody was all into it," Balboa said. And even though the excitement was palpable, they realized it was dangerous for a human to burrow into the layers of refuse in any garbage dump, much less a Third World dump where raw sewage was mixed with animal entrails, household waste, and all kinds of foul schmutz.

The snipers saw and smelled rotting food, goat guts, goat heads and blood, feces, rusted-out cans, gas canisters, "and just about everything you could think of" in their planned hiding area. "The smell was, I don't even know how to rate that. It's probably like your blue cheese mixed with the end-of-the-day smell at a slaughterhouse. Dried blood and guts and after sitting there a few weeks it ferments and you get the flies," Balboa said. "I was worried more about hepatitis or even malaria, there were flies everywhere."

They considered sitting directly in the trash but quickly discarded that idea.

"I didn't want to get any of that stuff near me," he said. "The other option was to use cold weather gear and ponchos and lay trash on top of us, with no dug out, just something in between us and the trash." They ended up adopting something closer to the second option, using a piece of plywood instead of poncho liners.

With two men for security, the sniper team was ferried by Stryker around the edge of the city from the desert side. They then walked into the trash pit under night vision optics from the cold, open desert, a moonlit trek of about a half-mile, far enough away that the vehicle drop-off would not have been noticed.

"We walked in from out in the middle of nowhere," he said.

Their plan was to dig a shallow pit on what looked like a mini-saddle with a downward slope in front. The pit would be wide enough for the four of them to lie prone on a slight, upward incline and look out toward the camera through a loophole in the strategically scattered trash. Their position would be hidden on either side by the two humps of trash and concealed in the rear by the backstop where their feet would rest.

For the walk-in, each of the four men either carried something or pulled security. They hauled two pieces of plywood, two two-by-fours, a shovel, and "everything we needed to be in there for three days." Each man was armed with an M4 rifle, and the sniper team had one M24 rifle that would lie between them in the hide.

They soon found their choice of shovel lacking. After pulling off the top layers of garbage with their noses wrinkled against the stench, they discovered the ground was rock-hard. Trying to dig with their shovel, a version of the e-tool with a small pick, was like using a plastic spoon to break up a pint of frozen ice cream.

"We thought it would take only a couple of hours to do our digging because we thought we'd just move the trash out of the way and then just dig a little. But the ground was so hard; it was dry, hard clay," Balboa said.

They started their unexpected hard labor at the front end of the hide, making it narrower toward the back where their feet would go. To say it was slow going would be an understatement. "Ridiculous" is how Balboa described it. They were working so hard and sweating so much, each man had to take several breaks to drink water.

"While three guys pulled security, one guy was digging real fast, breathing hard and heavy, and we did that rotation for like two hours, and we had only enough room for two guys. We were just really going at it," he said. "I couldn't believe this was happening. We're sitting here with all the trash moved out, but the ground is so hard. We did the best we could in the time we had."

Around 4 a.m., before first light caught up with them, the men decided to stop and get into position. The space, as it turned out, could only accommodate two men. It would be Balboa and their sniper section leader, Sgt. First Class Reyes Fernandez, whom they called "Fern."

"We did rock, paper, scissors to see who was going to go in there. My partner Gus lost, but he wasn't too worried, because it ended up raining and they were sitting in a building," Balboa said.

Fernandez and Balboa placed the plywood with the back end jammed into the backstop and propped it up as an overlay by placing a two-by-four near their shoulders and one by their lower legs. The rest of the wood was dug into the two side trash humps, and the whole thing was covered with the garbage they had removed earlier.

On the slit that looked out toward their objective, Balboa hung a discarded grain sack he found in the dump. It was great camouflage because it was perfectly fouled up like the rest of the detritus around them.

Before dawn, they had settled into their earthen hide, wearing their uniforms under their wet-weather pants and listening to the sounds around them, still keyed up from the nightlong activity of burrowing in. And there was that nervous exhilaration, "that sort of puckered-butt, hoping-nobody-saw-us feeling," Balboa said.

They weren't cold, yet. And they weren't wet, yet. They were just happy the plan had worked out mostly as they had wanted. Having the two men in a building over-watching their trashy position had actually turned out to be a better plan, as time would tell.

For the first few hours, they watched the camera and stayed alert, but the excitement of living like Oscar the Grouch started to fade. Around noon, it began to get cold and clouds rolled in.

It was autumn, around the time of Ramadan, the rainy season. Naturally, around 8 p.m., it started raining and continued to rain for eight hours. Now Fernandez and Balboa were lying on squishy wet ground with a puddle of putrid water creeping up beyond their boots.

The men began sharing their misery by radio, joking with each other about their hide sites. The smugness of having a dry building to sit in was gone for Gus and Brian because the roof had caved in under the weight of the rain. Balboa told them he couldn't take a shot even if he wanted to because he was shivering like a poodle.

And the prolonged exposure to the cold, wet ground was causing him to hesitate.

"I couldn't pee. We laughed about it later. After like the seventeenth hour, I started talking to my camera because I was getting delirious," Balboa said.

Besides the shivering cold, the culprit for his biological problem was a boulder he couldn't get away from that was pushing against his kidney. He scooched as far from it as he could, in Fernandez's direction, turned onto his side, and "went."

"So now I was laying in my own urine. That's the way it is. In sniper or recon, even in the infantry, you do things outside the box, mission or situation dictating, you put it out of the way. I've done spooning when I want to stay warm," he explained.

The urine wasn't that bad, he said. At least it was his. After the rain the sides of their hide started to deteriorate and little pieces of trash were seeping in, slithering down next to them. "I'd pick it up and throw it out the front or stuff it into the side, or I'd see something hanging that was all black and green and I was like, 'I don't even want to touch that,' so I'd shove it up in the crack like, 'Ew, what am I touching?' Probably somebody's, like, I just think the worst," he said, recalling the details with a scrunched face. "I'm like, this really sucks, this is not how I figured it to be. We were supposed to have a kill by now and get out of here, not stay here for a full three days."

But there they were on their second night. It was about twenty degrees, and their first unwanted guests showed up.

Fernandez and Balboa could hear some rustling behind them, some movement, but they couldn't see that it was a pack of about ten dogs rooting around with their noses. The guys in the building had eyes on them, and as the dogs went about their scavenging, they started to come around the sides and to the front of the hide. One of them lifted its head up and looked right at Balboa.

"I kind of made a little 'click' sound and looked him in the eye, and he ran off. To me it meant I did a really good job, because if the dogs didn't even know we were there and couldn't smell us, it was good," Balboa said. "It was that much more reinforced when the guy came and literally walked on the wood and our position."

It was a goatherd that the other team saw from about 1,500 meters out. As he slowly made his way closer over the course of an hour, the team watching him felt sure he was unarmed, but everyone was nervous. This was the perfect hide site; it wasn't supposed to be compromised.

The guys in the building on the radio told Balboa and Fernandez that "if the guy even flinches or farts sideways, we'll light him up."

Balboa and Fernandez prepared themselves by lying on their backs with their weapons at the ready between their legs and the soles of their feet on the plywood, positioned to kick it upward and come out guns blazing.

"The guy had his goats. He was just meandering and didn't know or think anything of it, and I'm like sweatin' bullets. We went silent on the radio; we're sitting there breathing heavy," Balboa said, estimating it was about 10 a.m.

The man wandered toward their hide. First the snipers heard rustling, then, footsteps. The man was walking on their plywood, and the snipers could hear him. Tension filled their hearts as the man bent down over the front of the hide.

"We see him, then we see a sandal, then another sandal, and we were like, 'This guy doesn't even know we're here.' He stepped right in front of our loophole, which was about twelve inches," Balboa said.

The man fished around in the right-side trash pile, then took another step down the gently sloping trash pile in front of the hide, putting himself about chest level with Balboa's M24, which was aimed at the man.

The goatherd squinted his eyes and focused on the crude opening, but the hide was dark so he couldn't tell what he was looking at. He stepped closer. Then he stepped closer again, craning his neck a little.

"Now he's like two feet out, and I stick my barrel right outside the grain sack, which is twelve inches from my face. I put my face out just enough so he could see it was an American soldier and an American gun. I didn't want him to think we were insurgents because some people care and would tell the Iraqi police who would come and shoot the place up," Balboa said.

Balboa gave him a slow nod, and the man quickly backed up and kept his gaze fixed on the American sniper. "His eyes got real big. He looked at us, backed up, and kind of walked away," he said. "I didn't say anything to him; once he saw the barrel, he knew."

The team in the building watched the goatherd mosey on down with his goats and go about his business. "He obviously didn't have any insurgency ties or tell anybody because we stayed there another twenty-four hours," Balboa said.

Dogs and goatherds aside, the team did eventually get a nibble near the bait. It was midafternoon on their second full day there, and they were still nervous they'd be overrun, not fully believing the goatherd was an innocent passerby. Even the chain of command knew they had been exposed but told them to stay put.

A young man drove up close to the pole where the camera was, riding a beat-up moped-style bike. Both teams had him in sight. The team in the building was about two hundred meters away but didn't have a good shot. So the trash team snipers said they'd take a shot from their four-hundred-meter position if the guy gave them cause.

"I have him in my crosshairs. He got off his bike, opened up the bike seat, took out what looked like a pistol, and cocked it. All he had to do was point it at the camera, and I would have been able to do my deal," Balboa said.

Instead, the man sat on his bike, looked at the device a couple of times, looked down, looked at it again, and either thought twice about it or got scared and drove off.

Shot denied. One more night in the pit.

Around midday the next day, the boys from A Company rumbled up to within four feet of the hide site in a Stryker vehicle and dropped the hatch for the snipers. By this time Fernandez and Balboa were close to hypothermia. And that wasn't all.

"They were hooting and hollering about coming to get us, and then when we got in there, they were like, 'Oh my God! You guys stink so bad,' like to the point where the whole ride back, guys who normally try to stay behind the slat armor because of the IEDs were hanging outside the hatch gagging and stuff," Balboa said.

As he headed toward the vehicle, he snapped a couple of pictures he could use later for training other guys.

The team wasn't happy about being extracted in daylight, but in keeping with the warning to any locals who might have been watching, the commanders wanted people in the area to see that their snipers could be hiding anywhere at any time.

For those idiots who might think the threat was gone and come in and shoot the camera anyway, the commanders left the building team in place to take care of them.

Balboa burned his uniform, cleaned his snivel and wet-weather gear, and washed the boots he'd been wearing for seven months, not wanting to discard a good pair of boots, even stinky ones.

"Even though we got compromised and we exfilled during the day, I still consider it to have been a very successful sniper mission. The only thing that didn't work out is we didn't get four guys in there," Balboa said. "The training aspect of it is thinking outside the box. You can only use buildings so many times."

By 2005, when they made their trash-pit hide site, he noted, a lot of American snipers had used a lot of hide sites in Mosul.

The trash pit was a new frontier for them.

"From that position we could see everything in front of us. We could see the corner where the cars came in, and we could almost see the building our buddies were in," he said. "I consider that to have been a success."

Hiding in the Wild, Wild East

Millions of miles were driven over the years on Iraq's roads by tens of thousands of uniformed and civilian road warriors who slipped behind the wheels of trucks, tractor trailers, and Humvees to keep the war machine supplied.

Tons of stuff like boots, bullets, and fuel; shampoo, chow, and water; vehicle parts, aircraft parts, and weapons parts was moved around on Iraq's main routes and secondary roads from Basra to Baghdad, Musayyib to Mosul, and Karbala to Kirkuk.

During the surge of 2007, when the number of troops in country was close to 150,000, the highest level of the war, more than 475,000 tons of food and several thousand tons more of construction material such as concrete barriers, steel, and wood were shipped to Kuwait from the Defense Supply Center in Philadelphia, then taken over land by truck hundreds of miles into Iraq.

It was a part of the war that rarely made the front page—or any page—of the newspaper in more than seven years of the U.S. presence in Iraq.

Still, that log train never stopped, even when the going got rough, even when the drivers and their security escorts were killed by crude, home-made bombs that exploded as they passed through, detonated by low-level cowards hiding in the shadows with cell phones and garage door openers.

The bombers didn't get as many as they might have, however, and lost a lot more of their own, denied their evil deeds by people like Sgt. Ray, a First Infantry Division sniper who did his part by killing several bomb emplacers on the main supply routes of eastern Baghdad and coming up with innovative ways to be where they least expected him.

"We were in a very sporting environment," he said of the area around Forward Operating Base Rustamiyah on the south side of the infamous Sadr City, a forsaken section on the east end of Iraq's capital whose more than one million residents were steeped in poverty, soaking in sewage, and surrounded by Mahdi army militiamen. Sadr City's troubles were many, and they spilled over its boundaries to feed a level of violence that refused to be tamed for years.

It was on the eastern and southern flanks of this part of the city, which looks like a perfectly rectangular grid when viewed on a satellite map, that Sgt. Ray and his team of snipers worked at night to watch over and keep safe the U.S. supply convoys that rumbled through.

The big supply routes—the north-south Route Pluto and the roughly east-west Route Predator—were like highway boulevards, split roads with two lanes on each side, divided by a canal, sewer trench, or concrete island of some sort.

Along that divider, the commander of Second Battalion, Sixteenth Infantry built a series of concrete observation towers in early 2007 about every quarter mile, with some standing sentry over traffic control points. From these makeshift towers, Iraqi police armed with AK-47 assault rifles could watch the traffic points and provide security for their counterparts on the ground. Except on the nights when snipers like Ray and his crew arrived.

"We would just pull the Iraqi police off the tower, get them to pile their cell phones into a corner and their AKs into another corner, tell them to pull out their mattresses, drink tea, smoke, whatever you want. We'd say, 'We got security tonight,' and it got to where we didn't even need an interpreter anymore. They would just get down and hand us their stuff," Sgt. Ray said. "They really enjoyed that."

And the Iraqis weren't the only ones who enjoyed it. Ray's security element, usually soldiers who didn't get a chance to get off the base much, welcomed the foreignness of hanging out with the Iraqis—while they kept an eye on them. "We would take supply clerks or someone from another company. They would drink tea with the Iraqis, have fun. For some reason soldiers like to drink tea," he said.

The snipers were grouped into two teams of five, with three people in each tower and two people on the ground. They only worked at night and never hid in the same tower twice in a row.

While the tea was brewing downstairs, Sgt. Ray and his team would watch for trouble brewing on the highway. The towers were really just six-foot-wide vertical culvert pipes with a ladder on the inside to climb the twenty feet to a circular ledge. From there the snipers could watch and take a shot from a standing or squatting position through little windows that measured about eighteen by twenty-four inches. Above them were eight more feet of pipe with a vented concrete seal at the top.

The main supply routes they had to keep bomb-free were two of the biggest in Baghdad, and notoriously bad for attacks. The sniper towers were something new, and they worked.

"We had to be very creative in how to use snipers in Iraq. You can't sit on top of someone's house because there could be retribution for the people who own the house. I built towers all over the place," said Lt. Col. Ralph Kauzlarich, commander of the 2-16 Infantry, a unit under the First Infantry Division's Fourth Brigade Combat Team.

"It was harassment, if you will. Psychologically it really scares the insurgents when someone gets shot and, believe me, everyone hears about it and they tend not to go into that area anymore."

At first, Sgt. Ray recalled, Kauzlarich was leery of sending his snipers out in sector without a full complement of infantrymen for security. But as the snipers found success and developed their own intelligence, they gained their commander's confidence.

"We did our research. We found what we thought was a dirty mosque. We set up around it and shot some people moving weapons in and out of the mosque. After that it became 'Okay, now you guys are starting to contribute to the battlefield,' so he took us off the security detail and kind of took the leash off for a couple of months," Ray said.

He placed his snipers in adjacent towers so they could have eyes on the same objective while covering for one another if something went wrong. They had multiple angles on the same target and the advantage of aerial surveillance from an aerostat blimp at their base, which gave them even more intelligence and a sharper, broader view of what they were seeing.

The wider roads in the east were the ones that could accommodate the size and speed of the larger supply trucks. Because of their location on the city's fringes, the roads were also magnets for bomb emplacers who, Sgt. Ray said, were more willing to take a chance to place their bombs on the highways than in the inner city.

"On the road you have plenty of area for shrapnel to land before it goes into friendly areas, so you'd see a higher percentage of devices on the open roads or a road next to a junkyard or soccer field than you would on a road with apartment buildings on both sides," he said.

The snipers ran the tower mission three times a week and took at least one shot every other week. They were up against the same types of bomb emplacers who had always been willing to do the job, disgruntled and desperate locals looking to make some money. But by the time Sgt. Ray's battalion got there in February 2007, a new and more deadly kind of bomb known as an EFP, or "explosively formed projectile," had been in use for at least a year.

The first improvised explosive devices, or IEDs, were mostly made of artillery rounds scrounged from the vast stockpiles left by Saddam Hussein's army. Those types of bombs are technically known as blast mines because the raw blast from the mass of explosives is what affects the target vehicle.

Later on, the enemy made the blast mine more effective by increasing the amount of explosives. But U.S. troops began seeing a more deadly device in 2006 when plastic explosives were placed on the back of a cone of metal, usually copper, and affixed to a roadside tree or a guardrail at the height of a Humvee door. When detonated, the force of the blast inverted the cone to form almost a dart of superheated metal capable of penetrating even very substantial armor.

While the city was under curfew in the early morning hours, miles-long convoys with the heaviest trucks barreled through on the darkened roads that skirted that eastern edge of Baghdad, their drivers praying they could dodge those EFPs.

"I had a very specific area that I had to control and make sure it remained EFP-free. The dumb bad guys would make themselves available to get a bullet, and we would provide them with one. On the road at night, we'd see them down there, and we'd shoot them out of their sandals," Kauzlarich said.

The tower missions had a direct effect on the safety of the convoys, and violence on the roads was kept at bay. But an even more important part of guarding the truckers, and more difficult in its execution, was the job of going after the insurgent nerve centers to kill or capture the elusive bomb makers, the bomb planters, and the men who made it all possible with money, supplies, and more money.

Those larger-scale missions were planned and executed by the battalion—sometimes in concert with another nonmilitary government agency—and a larger complement of infantrymen and air assets, depending on the size of the operation.

Sgt. Ray, who was reluctant to use his full name, in part to secure his family's privacy and safety, played his role as a sniper in support of those secret direct-action missions, nighttime raids on the homes of known high-value targets.

The 2-16 Infantry arrived in its area of operations and wasted no time in hitting back with a strong show of manpower and a willingness to crush the violence, as the surge intended. After a few raids in which the suspects were either killed or captured, a spate of direct fire attacks on the infantry's base would happen like clockwork.

"Every time we shot or captured someone big like a finance guy or a bomb maker, the locals shot rockets at us twenty-four hours later," Sgt. Ray said. The attacks were generally lame, but the attackers were predictable in their timing, so the sniper section hatched a plan to go after them.

The local thugs, presumably hired by the henchmen of the captured or dead guy, were firing their rockets from trucks driven onto a field near the Diyala River. Surrounded by high ground, the field was a good launch site. But there was a weak point, and Sgt. Ray and his boys found it on a satellite map. One side of the field was open to the river, on the other side of which was a wide-open area where the snipers could easily hide and probably get a clear shot.

There was only one small hitch they had to overcome.

Because commanders in Iraq each had a specific area of operations delineated by a dark line on a map, simply crossing the river into another guy's territory was dangerous—unless that commander knew about the mission—because it could lead to U.S. troops firing on each other.

Even though it was during the height of the troop surge, the commander in charge of the area across the river was stretched thin for manpower and considered the area near the river—the farthest edge of his section of operations—quiet. And it was, which made it perfect for the snipers. The guys launching the rockets from the field assumed there would be no risk of getting caught as they rarely saw an American patrol on the other side of the river.

After an exchange of messages between the commanders clearing the way for the sniper op, the snipers waited to launch.

Using the same satellite map, they had chosen what seemed to be a good hide site, a natural depression in the earth that looked as if it could have been an old, worn crater from a rocket or a bomb. It appeared to be practically isolated except for two small villages on either side.

It was around 10 p.m. the first time they went there. Bravo Company had captured someone of interest so the likelihood of a rocket launch looked probable.

The snipers left their base with five gun trucks armed with a long-range advanced scout surveillance system and a .50-caliber machine gun and crossed the river on a bridge a few miles south of their crater. They took Route Crow, a main road north, and at a bend in the road, the patrol slowed down so the sniper contingent could slip out while the Humvees kept rolling about a mile past the crater.

Still an unknown, the crater, which they had only seen on a satellite map, ended up being pretty good. It was about three feet deep and twelve feet wide, enough space for the six men on the team—two shooters; Sgt. Ray, the team leader, on scope; and three men—to watch the network of trails behind them.

The soil was soft, "kind of like Midwestern topsoil," Ray said, and the hole was symmetrical, with a lot of grass around it that would help conceal them. They infiltrated the site by following the river right to it.

Behind them were Route Crow and a network of footpaths to an open area. There was a trail between the two quiet, sparsely populated villages, which were about two hundred meters apart, much closer than they looked on the map. The snipers' hide site was dead center between the little clusters of houses.

"It was really a luck game," Sgt. Ray said. But it worked out perfectly for the first night's mission, though not the mission they expected. The enemy launched no rockets, but the snipers shot two guys laying a bomb on the main road into Bravo Company's combat outpost.

"It wasn't the target we wanted, but an equally important target," he said.

Buoyed by their success, they pulled the crater mission four more times and were able to nail it at least twice when the rocket assailants were there, killing an unknown number of them. They also isolated and captured a rocket truck.

They started infiltrating at night ahead of planned raids or snatch missions and stayed hidden in the crater for a full day, doing the part of the job some outsiders might think of as the glamorous part. It was summer, and the weather in the crater was hot and uncomfortable. The beating sun soared to 120 degrees and baked the soldiers into their body armor as they lay flat and waited for nightfall. "We couldn't drink a lot of water. There's nowhere to urinate, and you can only carry so much, maybe three quarts for an all-day affair," Ray said.

The snipers had wanted to wear something other than what Sgt. Ray called their "glow-in-the-dark ACUs," but they didn't receive permission. "We're not Special Forces, we're just a regular unit. We asked for bongo trucks and local vehicles and asked to dress like Iraqis over our body armor, and we were told that would put the locals in danger," he said. "Erring on the side of safety, if we did get contact, I'd rather have armor on me than nothing. We shot in helmets, we shot in full kit."

They put branches and leaves on top of a thin canvas Sgt. Ray had, and as uncomfortable as they were in biding their time, the missions at night went off without a hitch.

Until the fifth mission. And it happened to be the one in which they took a new platoon leader with them to show him just how dangerous their work can be.

"I was trying to show him what we do, show him how we move," Sgt. Ray said. "He thought we were lazy because he'd only seen us on the raids. He thought we went over the top of a rooftop and laid down. He hadn't seen our sniper-only missions before."

A crazy infiltration route and a dose of humble pie contributed greatly to the young lieutenant's education on snipers. "We wanted to break him off so we gave him the .50-cal and two magazines of ammo. He was carrying about sixty-nine pounds on top of his body armor," Ray said.

They started their infiltration by being dropped off three roads farther away from their usual point on Route Crow and approached the crater site in a big, sweeping U-shaped route before making a bold five-kilometer hump to get into place.

"We hit every irrigation ditch, every sewer ditch, every uneven terrain we could possibly find," said Sgt. Ray, who was point man and as such was the first to arrive at Route Crow where he took a knee and checked security like a hawk before pushing across with his team. As he performed his stop-look-listen drill, Ray didn't notice right away what the lieutenant was up to. Exhausted and demonstrating just how wet he was behind the ears, the lieutenant decided he would take a little rest.

"He did a rucksack flop like he was in Ranger School instead of taking a knee and pulling his weapon up and pulling security in his sector. He just laid down like a parachute landing and was using his rifle as a back rest as he pulled out his canteen," Sgt. Ray said. "I had to go over and slap him upside the head and tell him, 'This is the real deal,' that he had to take a knee like everybody else. We had a lot of problems with this particular lieutenant, but he started to realize there's more to being a sniper than just laying on a rooftop."

And then the officer got his next lesson in sniping—how a hide site gets compromised.

After the team crossed Route Crow and moved through a series of cornfields below one of the little nearby villages, it settled into the crater, which had become wonderfully familiar by now, almost too good to be true.

Lying in their usual positions, one of the guys told Sgt. Ray that there was "something funny" over by his place. It was funny—like an exploding cigar. "It was a 155 mm artillery round with a wire sticking out right in the middle of our circle. So it was time to go," Ray said.

He cut the wires on the bomb, and they all made a run for the gun trucks after calling for a ride home, leaving the crater for the last time, their newly educated platoon leader in tow.

The tower missions continued after that, and the only time it got quiet, Sgt. Ray said, was during an unexpected cease-fire called by Mahdi army leader Moqtada al-Sadr in August 2007 that was supposed to last six months.

But for Sgt. Ray, the quiet wouldn't last that long. Within a week of the announced cease-fire, after eight months in country, he was being medically evacuated following his miraculous survival of an EFP attack that critically wounded two other soldiers in his Humvee.

It happened on September 2 when, after a night of training at a firing range a few clicks away from their own base on Route Brewer, Ray and some of the other snipers decided to combine a reconnaissance mission at daybreak with a run for breakfast at Forward Operating Base Loyalty just west of Sadr City, where the chow hall was superior to their own.

Taking the usual security precautions, the group of snipers rolled out of the firing range around 6 a.m. in four Humvees with the intention of videotaping the route to FOB Loyalty so they could study it later for possible new hide sites.

Sgt. Ray rode shotgun, which he hated. He is taller than six foot five inches, which might not matter in a roomy, commercially sold Hummer, but in a tactical Humvee, the front passenger seat is crammed with stuff like a computer screen that, among other things, tracks "blue" or friendly forces, and a bulky radio console. On top of that, the seat is not readily adjustable.

He rode with his knees up to his chest.

A rarity in the sniper community, Ray had been a member of the Presidential Escort Platoon in the Third Infantry Regiment's Old Guard at Fort Myer in Arlington, Virginia, for almost three years before being assigned to the 2-16 Infantry.

"I was one of the sword guys," he said of his first duty assignment. He was also one of the short guys. "Our group was six-foot-six to six-foot-nine. If you were shorter than six-foot-five, you were kicked out of our platoon."

During his assignment in the Old Guard, Sgt. Ray did missions like Ronald Reagan's funeral in 2004 and George W. Bush's second inauguration in 2005. He did general officer retirements at the Pentagon, and state dinners and head of state visits at the White House, and he lined the perimeter of the Rose Garden with the Marines during presidential speeches.

"We were the lawn statues, the pretty boys standing out in the grass," he said. He volunteered to walk the solemn vigil at the Tomb of the Unknowns at Arlington National Cemetery when the platoon in charge of that mission had its Christmas party. All the while he educated himself on the art of sniping by reading everything he could.

Ray was only too happy to leave behind the trappings and duties of Washington's ceremonial life to do his part in Baghdad, and as the four Humvees weaved their way through the serpentine wire barriers at a checkpoint on Route Brewer that early morning, he was brutally cut down by the same guys he hunted at night.

"We took nine EFPs into our truck," Sgt. Ray said, still amazed that he was alive years later to tell about it.

Two projectiles burned through underneath the dash, piercing the blue force tracker and his radio, knocking them out; one stopped in his ballistic glass window; one went into the air intake and one into the engine; one went through his door and burned into his stomach, and another sliced across his back and took off the sniper's leg in the seat behind him; one flew past his chest and took off the 40 mm grenades on his vest before taking off his gunner's leg and zipping under the driver's arms above his lap and out the door on the other side; and the last one hit the gun turret. A tenth projectile grazed the top of the cab.

"I thought I was dead, I thought I was cut in half and bleeding out at the time," he said. "I refused to let them take care of me because you don't treat the dead."

Sgt. Ray had an EFP stuck between his armor plate and his groin pad. The searing hot projectile had burned through the groin pad and one of those big riggers belts.

"I felt that heat and thought that heat was the feeling of something going straight through me, and I didn't want them to drag my body out and leave my legs in the truck," he said.

The whole time the mayhem inside the Humvee was unfolding, the gun trucks were being attacked with small arms fire from behind concrete walls. The 240B machine guns the soldiers were fighting back with were not able to penetrate the wall. So the snipers went to the tail hatch of their Humvees and pulled out their Barrett .50-caliber rifles, which punched right through the walls, killing more than fifteen enemy fighters.

In the attack, Ray was struck by the door handle to his right, which hit the sheath of his femoral artery and had to be surgically removed from his hip. Another of the copper slugs seared a hole the size of a large hand through his groin pad just below his belly button and burned its way through flesh and fat to the muscle layer. The muscle and flesh from his right hip to his spine were burned through by another slug that came in through his side armor plate and deflected off his back plate. Plus, he had a concussion and his arm was broken in three places.

The snipers never got breakfast that morning, and Sgt. Ray was medically retired by the Army because of his injuries.

He's not sure how many rocket guys were killed from the crater hide site, but the enemy stopped using the field as a launch pad for their direct fire missions. Instead, they began launching mortars from somewhere inside the city.

"We enjoyed the fact that they thought they had a safe spot because the other unit never patrolled over there," Sgt. Ray said. The team had effectively denied the rocket launchers their terrain and forced them to resort to a more inaccurate way of attacking.

He didn't get to do everything he wanted in the Army, like trying out for Special Forces or continuing to work as a sniper. But Sgt. Ray made a difference to the road warriors who drove their tons of supplies all over Iraq for years after he left.

WITNESS TO CONTROVERSY

In July 2002, less than a year into U.S. operations in Afghanistan, a secret operation was planned to bring in a high-level Taliban leader.

He was known to frequently visit his ancestral home in the village of Deh Rawood, about 250 miles southwest of Kabul in Uruzgan province.

Men from Army, Navy, and Air Force Special Operations units were brought in from other areas of the country to take part in the major operation, which would unfold over the course of a few days before a well-timed snatch-and-grab raid took place.

Air support for the ground operation included an AC-130 gunship and a B-52 bomber, and in the ridgelines around the village, teams of snipers, observers, and communications specialists would burrow in and generate intelligence in the days leading up to it.

"Our job in a situation like that was not to interdict the target in question. Our job was to observe and to report and to corral anyone who tried to come through the mountain passes and attempted to escape," said Sgt. First Class Ricky, a sniper with the Third Special Forces Group.

He, several Navy SEALs, and other Third Group snipers were on different teams of eight to twelve men that were broken down into smaller teams and positioned on adjacent mountain ridges a few hundred meters apart. They could see the passes nearest their hides, and they could also see the same things in the village from different angles.

Deh Rawood is a cluster of small village compounds on a valley floor at about eight thousand feet in elevation where a pattern of streams and irrigation canals flows near the larger Helmand River running through the valley. About 1,500 meters away and above the valley, the observing and reporting teams were tucked strategically into the ridgelines.

"The village is more urban in the center and starts to get more rural out to about six hundred to one thousand meters to the base of the mountains. There were a lot of irrigation ditches in the fields, and on the back side of the mountains, there were vast opium fields. They would bring all the opium to this village for sale and move it down the rivers," Sgt. First Class Joey, another sniper with the Third Special Forces Group, said.

The teams infiltrated at 10 p.m. by helicopter, far enough away that the sounds of the helicopters' rotor blades chopping through the air wouldn't compromise the mission before it even started. They then embarked on a sweaty, punishing slog on hardscrabble terrain for at least two miles, each man carrying three or four gallons of water, which weighs twenty-four to thirty-two pounds, and humping rucksacks filled with not only what they would need to live without resupply for the duration of the mission, like food, but also radio equipment, batteries, and the munitions they would need for the fight. Each human pack mule was carrying more than one hundred pounds.

"It doesn't sound like a long walk, but in that kind of terrain and carrying that kind of weight, it's slow because of the rocks and steep terrain," Sgt. First Class Ricky said. "You're carrying guns, everyone's under night vision, and you're walking all night until damn near when the sun comes up."

That kind of trekking with that amount of gear would lay the average person out for days. But on a mission at war, where the timing of the teams' arrival on the ridges was critical and being compromised would mean certain disaster, there was no room for a weak link. Every man was physically fit and capable of carrying his own weight. Everyone was switched on high, and the level of adrenaline pumping meant the men had to force themselves to chill out after the extreme feat of just getting there.

"In that situation, for the first forty-four to forty-eight hours, you really have to make guys lay down because they want to stay up, they want to see what's going on. They're jacked up from the infil, and you have to tell them, 'Hey, go lay down, get some sleep man, because your turn is coming and in eight hours my ass is going to sleep,'" Sgt. First Class Joey said.

Now that the challenge of reaching the hide site without getting caught was finished, a well-rehearsed chaos began with the swift unpacking of gear and each man finding his place to settle into the craggy ground before sunrise.

They had to become a part of the landscape, go into still-life mode by either lying down or crouching in the rocks, moving very slowly and avoiding positions that would create a silhouette against the sun. Succumbing to primitive caveman desires to start a fire was out of the question.

"We like our jobs and doing what we do. It definitely takes a different kind of person to sit up there for days on end in Indian land watching over targets with bad guys walking all over the place and trying to figure out who's bad and who's not," Sgt. First Class Ricky said.

Goatherds, he said, may not walk right up to the hide site, but they may see it and the sniper has to figure out his next move. "Now you have to weigh the risk. He's fifty meters away. Do we lay here or do we freakin' bug out, what do we do?" Sgt. First Class Ricky said. "I've been lucky, I've rolled the dice a time or two, and he either didn't see us or he didn't tell anybody he saw us."

And there were the more stressful tasks of resting, sleeping, biding time, and keeping calm, which take the patience and maturity of seasoned operators who can endure the restrictive and uncomfortable environment in the intimate company of a bunch of other people.

It was rocky, and the wind could turn a man's skin to leather. When the sun went down, the temperature dropped more than twenty degrees, which, after a humid ninety-degree day, made for a frigid night under the stars.

Basic bodily needs, like eating and eliminating waste, were not afterthoughts. In fact, for some it was a tactical art form.

"That's part of the reason we go through all this training like Ranger School and some of the other schools that deprive you of sleep and food. You just learn to operate under those types of conditions," said Sgt. First Class Ricky. When people are lying in a hide site for several days, they move so little that the urge to eat is lessened—and so are its effects.

"I'll tell you what we did for sanitation. We would pop Imodium, and it stops you up so you don't have to defecate for five days. Of course when you get back, that's a whole 'nother story," he said with wide eyes and a convincing nod.

As the hours turned to days and the moon and the sun came and went, layers of different priorities were at work around the clock and each team member had a specific task. The sensitive operation involved communicating with the other services and coordinating reports on what they were seeing.

"You had guys on glass looking at targets, you had guys on the computer making products to send back, you had guys taking photos and uploading them into the computer and labeling them with a new labeling system," Sgt. First Class Joey said, explaining that over the course of the snipers' many deployments to the war zone, the digital equipment they used for observation and reconnaissance grew increasingly more sophisticated. They had to learn it all, sometimes while on the job.

Some guys did old-fashioned sketching with one hand, while with the other hand, they used the latest laser range finders to build quick-reference range cards in case they had to take a shot.

At a distance of 1,500 meters from the village center, the Special Operations teams weren't at firing range and they couldn't identify individual faces, but they could see a lot of other things, like routine human activities and obvious hostile actions; they could see guns and the types of vehicles coming and going from the village complex.

The teams used a tagging system to give every vehicle a code and tracked parked and returning vehicles, how long they stayed, who was in them, whether they carried guns and what kind, and whether the vehicles were loaded or unloaded and when.

"We tracked just every little detail, all things, and we might follow a particular car of interest. There was a road that skirted the outside of the village into this flat area and continued up into the mountains. If the car moved past our position, we could pass it off to the other teams, and everybody picked up and had eyes on. If it eventually disappeared, we could pass it off to an air asset," Sgt. First Class Joey said.

The operation to catch the Taliban leader had been postponed a few times before the teams were mobilized, so there was a lot of hurry up and wait in the days before they infiltrated their mountain positions.

Postponement of an operation is a classic war zone occurrence caused by a lot of factors, like the availability or condition of people and equipment, the weather, or a change in the intelligence landscape.

After the operation began and everyone was in place, several days passed with no evidence of the man's presence, like a sighting of his usual entourage.

But on their fourth day in the hide sites, the teams did witness what became one of the earliest controversies for the American military in Afghanistan, when the AC-130 circling overhead in support of the ground operation fired upon the village in what became known as "the wedding party bombing," though there was no wedding and the attack was provoked, the Special Forces snipers said, by militants on the ground foolishly eager to shoot down a mighty American gunship.

During the Vietnam era, counterinsurgency doctrine took shape as leaders realized that the way to beat an insurgency was to dry up its source of support by winning over the people. The focus shifted from dominating terrain and the enemy to controlling the "human terrain."

Tactical operations, however, must be directed at strategic goals, and although the tactical focus on the human terrain did feed the strategic goal of counterinsurgency, America was defeated by the shift in public opinion against the effort. The North Vietnamese commanding general, Vo Nguyen Giap, said in a 1989 interview with Morley Safer as excerpted in *The Vietnam War: An Encyclopedia of Quotations*, written by Howard Langer and published by Greenwood Press in 2005, "The war was fought on many fronts. At that time the most important one was American public opinion."

In the current wars, America's enemies had realized early on that they could capitalize on any collateral damage that might be inflicted by U.S. forces by feeding images to the Western media. It was a short jump from there to planning operations to produce images that would garner the desired media effect. American military leaders lagged behind in realizing the shift in the center of gravity, which gave the enemy the opportunity to exploit what happened that night.

"There was an air strike because there were antiaircraft in that village trying to shoot down American aircraft," Sgt. First Class Ricky said.

After the AC-130 fired upon the village to take out the antiaircraft positions the snipers had seen, the first reports that reached the media claimed that the Americans had bombed a wedding party and killed three hundred people who were simply firing their rifles in the air to celebrate the marriage. The Taliban seized on the possibility of exploiting the media and turned a tactical defeat into a strategic victory.

"As far as I'm concerned," Ricky said, "it was just a ruse for them, a scapegoat to say the reason they were shooting was celebratory fire, which is bullcrap."

A senior Army spokesman and Afghan officials who went to the village within forty-eight hours of the attack in the summer of 2002 reported that the attack more accurately had killed around thirty and injured sixty and that a bomb was never dropped. "The B-52 never engaged," the Army spokesman said eight years after the event, citing what he could of classified reports on the event. "If it had engaged, there would have been a giant crater. But that's almost irrelevant. People were killed, that's all they knew. It just wasn't nearly as many as they had said, and there was no wedding."

The military never disputed the shooting by the AC-130. A joint American and Afghan investigation later reported that something akin to a bridal shower had been going on in one of the buildings and when the shooting started, a lot of people, including the women, ran outside and became mingled with the antiaircraft shooters, who were also running for cover.

But the report of a bombed wedding party persisted, mostly because there were no independent observers on the objective, a pattern that repeated itself as the war in Afghanistan continued through the decade.

American and coalition troops learned that their ruthless enemy had no regard for the Law of War, which is after all essentially a gentlemen's agreement between nation states that it has no stake in. The enemy regularly used its own people as human shields, launching attacks from "protected" targets such as schools, mosques, or even a group of innocent civilians, knowing that not only would civilians be killed when the uniformed forces responded, but also that the images they produced would be broadcast around the world.

Immediately following those provoked attacks, the enemy issued its own news releases showing images of dead civilians, including children. Too salacious for the international media to ignore, images of the carnage, such as the alleged wedding party, were quickly posted, and the Taliban's version of events was reported without all the surrounding facts.

The Taliban in Afghanistan, with its own official spokesman and Web site, gained superiority on the stage of public opinion as the U.S. military slowly worked to change the way it disseminated its own information, sometimes by embedding journalists with units undertaking large operations. But with aviation resources in Afghanistan stretched thin, it was not always possible to get the media to remote outposts, nor was the media always there in large enough numbers.

Sgt. First Class Ricky and Sgt. First Class Joey said that in four days of watching the village of Deh Rawood, they saw no activity that would have indicated a wedding, including celebratory fire. What they did see that night was, instead, a barrage of fire and tracers coming from 14.5 mm antiaircraft guns, aimed at the American aircraft circling overhead.

"It's the tactic of the enemy. They know our weakness is political correctness," Sgt. First Class Ricky said.

The role of the ridgeline teams, he said, was primarily one of observing and reporting, so when the American pilots asked for confirmation that they were being shot at, the teams not only confirmed it but indicated which courtyards the shooting was coming from.

"We on the ground did not clear weapons hot for pilots or anything. They said, 'Hey, we're being shot at,' and the rules of engagement back then were a lot more lax," Sgt. First Class Ricky recalled. "When you have a Spectre gunship flying around up there, they know they're being shot at and they know where it's coming from. They just double-tapped with our information."

As it turns out, the Taliban leader they were seeking was not caught that night, even though the teams had what they considered to be reliable intelligence that he would be there to attend a big meeting.

"We saw plenty of antiaircraft guns, plenty from my vantage point. And there were tons of guys carrying AK-47s around. Obviously if there is antiaircraft shooting, there are bad people there," Sgt. First Class Joey said.

Making matters stickier for the Americans was the relationship between the leaders of the conventional and the unconventional sides of the Army, which back in 2002 didn't share information as readily or even work together as partners as they did later on. The details of what soldiers like Sgt. First Class Ricky and Sgt. First Class Joey knew they had seen that night were not relayed to regular Army investigators trying to set the record straight.

The tragedy of the civilian casualties lingered, but the attack had effectively cleared the village, if not the man they were seeking.

"We definitely killed a lot of bad guys, just not the bad guy we were after. When the cleanup crew rolled in there, they rolled into that guy's home and stayed there and wound up keeping a presence there. When I went back the next year, that was the house I stayed in for six months," Sgt. First Class Joey said.

The military's operational methods and the rules of engagement shifted as each new four-star general came in to manage the war in Afghanistan, but the sting of the wedding party faded only a little as time passed.

"Those civilian casualties were a black eye on us and what we were trying to do over there," said Sgt. First Class Ricky.

CHAPTER SIX

The Long Shot

Joe LeBleu

THE BONEYARD WAS A STRANGE, GHOSTED PLACE. IT WAS A BARE, EERIE wasteland of looted factories. There were a few villages in close proximity, and along with the water buffalo, you'd see donkeys and goats meandering about. Oddly, you'd often see dead goats near a dam south of the Boneyard, on both sides of a concrete bridge spanning the Euphrates.

Before I crashed that night, I slipped my map into the left cargo pocket of my desert bottoms and walked outside, staring at the night sky. I was mentally preparing myself to be back in combat, even though I knew it was only a leaders' recon. I remember telling myself, "Here we go. Round two, back into the eye of the hurricane."

I had to be at Captain Kirkpatrick's hootch at eight, and I wasn't much of a breakfast person, especially with the scent of sewage choking me in the gray early morning. Not being much of a coffee drinker, the morning aroma of the desert was my cup of joe. Hey, I'm grateful for such gifts as that fragrant aroma of Fallujah—an absolutely righteous scent indeed. Reminded me that I was still alive. Sans java, I went over to Martin's hootch at the Scouts and told him, "Grab Robi and let's roll."

Martin said, "Okay," then yelled, "Robi, get your shit—we're going," and we headed to the Humvee. I jumped in the back with my SR-25 and a 20-round magazine of 7.62x51mm 118LR jacked in, and two other magazines. I also carried my sidearm with three 15-round magazines. I wanted to be in the back so that I could have sufficient elevation to scan in front of our Humvee and our convoy.

Martin rode shotgun as Robi took the wheel, setting his M4 to the right side, a lesson learned from our first ambush in early September. I was alone in the back. It was terribly hot, a choking heat, with brilliant blue skies on all horizon lines. The mirage was heavy that day. I banged on the plywood and said, "Let's roll." We moved out toward 10th Mountain's command post, linked up with Captain Kirkpatrick, and went over last-minute details on the reconnaissance route, making sure everybody was on the same page. His last words at the briefing before we mounted up in the Humvees were, "Everybody be careful out there." Captain Kirkpatrick was cool and professional as always; in truth, he was the best company commander I saw in combat in Iraq.

We headed outside the wire, moving toward the city, and started our reconnaissance on dirt roads away from the Cloverleaf. Going down these dirt roads, just as I did during all missions in Fallujah, I remember taking more mental pictures, a sort of personal "photographic" field intelligence, marking key mosques and buildings in my memory. As with most missions, you could feel the apprehension in the air, but on this particular morning, the tension was as heavy as the smoke and the ever-present stench of goat manure and sewage.

The locals gave us hate stares and seemed especially distant. The usual aromas in the air were thicker that morning, more potent than usual. One strange thing I'd noticed is that right before we'd get hit, the smells usually became much stronger the deeper we'd get into Fallujah. By this time, I'd gained what most combat vets refer to as "the sixth sense." Once you've seen significant action, you can tell when something is wrong or when something is about to happen in combat. I had that same feeling now that I'd had in the Rangers before coming under fire—a certain feeling in my gut right before being ambushed.

I began shouting back and forth with Martin when I'd see a pile of trash or a group of suspicious people on a corner, and he'd respond, "I got it." I remember thinking to myself how strangely everyone was acting and how empty the streets and alleys were, key indicators for a fight. Robi was quiet and cool behind the wheel. Maybe Utah was on his mind, who knows, or he may have been hearing a Frankie Valli song; nonetheless, he was solid, eyes on, with his head in the game.

We started rolling northwest for the Boneyard, skirting the southern edges of Fallujah, dust trailing behind us. We were second in the convoy, following a 10th Mountain Humvee with a .50 cal mounted. Our trail Humvee was mounted with a MK19 40mm grenade launcher. One thing about 10th Mountain that impressed me: They were always loaded for bear. Their light infantrymen never hesitated to carry shotguns in Fallujah, for instance, which are ideal weapons for guerrilla warfare in jungle terrain and on urban turf in a desert environment, such as the tight alleys and jammed streets of Fallujah.

Sweat was pouring, and I remember thinking, *I hope we're not out here too much longer because I didn't bring any water.* By this point, I'd been training my body to survive for long periods of time in the desert without water. But this mission was extremely hot. We snaked back onto the main dirt road leading to the Boneyard, away from the mud huts and concrete villas that we'd just passed. As we started to pull away from the village on the main dirt road, I scanned ahead through the clouds of dust to ensure we were still on our route. Perhaps 500 meters west, a white pickup truck approached from the south, rolling slowly through crowds on both sides of a dirt road, heading north.

The lead 10th Mountain Humvee, with "Ma Deuce," the M2 .50-caliber heavy machine gun on point, now pulled ahead of us, at least 50 meters, making a huge gap in the convoy. I shouted, "Close the gap!" and Robi punched it. The next thing I knew, all was blackness and smoke and my ears were ringing and I remember the back of the Humvee lifting up off of the ground, throwing me to the front of the bed, and slamming me into Martin's back. Somehow I pulled myself together quickly, got my bearings, and dropped down, taking a knee in the back of the Humvee, dropping my chin to my chest as the shock and blast of the IED slammed the Humvee down on the dirt road, dust thick in the air.

Strangely enough, and quite fortunately, I knelt over my scope. I know of no reason why I did this, but I guess it was a gut feeling. One of my instincts was always, "If you protect your glass (scope), you will always be able to see your target."

My ears were ringing harder and louder than they had from any other IED blasts. This one felt ten times stronger. What seemed an eternity was probably only about thirty seconds, just enough time for me to get my bearings back. When I came to, I immediately started scanning 360 degrees, looking for a triggerman. By this point, I had learned from field intelligence that there would always be triggermen at least 300 meters from any IED ambush site. Once I'd completed my quick 360-degree scan, I turned to my team, to make sure they weren't wounded or dead.

I was looking through the black smoke rising around the rest of the convoy behind me. At that time, I'd seen a massive crater—I remember thinking, *A Humvee could fit in this crater*—and that's when we found out that there were three daisy-chained 155mm artillery rounds in the IED that had damn near killed us. At this point in the Iraq War, the insurgents were becoming more clever with how they were emplacing IEDs; for instance, in this ambush, they'd dug into the road itself, placed the IED, and then repaved the road, to the point where it looked like any normal road in Fallujah. This was a very different tactic than they'd used previously, where they'd just placed IEDs in trash on the side of roads, camouflaged with burlap sacks and rocks, or inside the carcass of a dead horse, dog, or donkey (even inside human corpses).

The radio was hot with calls for accountability: "Get a status report, get a status report!" was coming over our radio in the Humvee. We noticed crowds building up and people on rooftops behind us, in the village we'd just passed, some 300 meters to our rear. By this time, the lead 10th Mountain vehicle had turned around and was hauling ass to get back and help us.

We turned the whole convoy around and quickly got into a herringbone formation. Now the former trail Humvee with the Mark 19 became the lead vehicle, on point for the convoy, and the .50 cal mounted Humvee became trail vehicle, on rear guard for the convoy.

We'd maneuvered ourselves to the left side of the road so that the MK19's fields of fire were covering us. We did this so that I could maintain a direct line of sight west down the road, with my SR-25 set up on its bipod legs on top of the platform above the cab of the Humvee. The crowd was west of us, roughly 300 meters up ahead, and moving toward us. Now I could see a white pickup truck rolling away from the crowd, heading north. Scoping the truck, scanning now, I could see the wooden handgrips of AK-47 Kalashnikov assault rifles carried by men in dark *dishdashas* in the bed of the white truck.

Insurgents.

I yelled to the MK19 gunner in the lead vehicle, "Take out that white truck! Shoot the white truck—it's getting away!"

The MK19 gunner from 10th Mountain did not fire.

A 10th Mountain sergeant ran up to the gunner and started chewing his ass, saying, "What the fuck is wrong with you! Why didn't you shoot that truck?"

The gunner was frozen on the MK19, staring into space, his hands wrapped around the triggers. He didn't reply. The sergeant grimaced and pointed left, to a field south of us, and shouted, "Fire your goddamn weapon!"

The gunner fired two rounds from the MK19, into the open farmer's field, in front of a small mud house. The sergeant glared at the gunner and said, "Now you know how to pull the fuckin' trigger! Get back on point. If you see that fuckin' white pickup truck again, you had better fuckin' ventilate the motherfucker!"

The gunner looked down, morose and with eyes downcast, and muttered, "Roger, Sergeant."

What the fuck was that? I said to myself. I turned to Martin, laughing. "I think 10th Mountain just did a live-fire test fire."

I remember thinking, *Why haven't we taken AK fire yet?* This was standard operating procedure for IED ambushes in Fallujah. I said to Martin, "Don't you think it's weird that we haven't taken fire yet?" He raised his eyebrows, wincing, and said, "Yeah, it *is* weird," as he scanned the rooftops around us.

The crowd to the west had become a rolling mob. It had surged fast, and the road was full of Iraqis moving slowly toward us, dust boiling up all over the street. Some of the men had their faces and heads completely covered by black *khaffiyehs*; others wore red *khaffiyehs*, wrapped ninja-style around their heads, with only their eyes showing through my scope. For a split second, I thought, *Fuckin' Mogadishu all over again*, remembering what my brothers went through in Somalia on October 3, 1993, and the waves of mobs that had killed Shughart and Gordon when they saved Durant's life.

I dialed the dope into my scope at 300 meters, preparing for a shot. Looking through my scope, I called out to a 10th Mountain officer, whom I'd just seen out of the corner of my eye. "We've got a pretty big crowd building 300 meters west," I said. The officer was hustling down the right side of our convoy, headed right for me. He looked at the mob as I looked through my scope, my SR-25 set up on its bipods, resting on the plywood. I could feel his reluctance and thought, *This guy's hesitating when there is no time to hesitate.* At that second, I made the call.

"Check it out, sir. I can put a round at the edge of a building at the end of the street, at the corner, which will spray concrete in the direction of the crowd, all over their faces. That will push them back."

He looked at me quizzically and replied, "You can do that?"

"Roger," I said.

"Do it," he said.

I yelled to Robi, "Kill the engine!" Our Humvee was still set in, with the engine running hard, and as I looked through my scope, the vibration was throwing off my shot, shaking my rifle. Once the engine was quiet, I got back in a firing position, my right cheek resting on the stock, and eyed the crowd through my scope. I took a deep breath—your first breath is always your relaxation breath, to calm you—and exhaled slowly, feeling myself calm down from the adrenaline rush of the IED ambush. As I took my second breath and started to exhale, I zeroed in on a crack that I could see, running dark and jagged down the brown-painted concrete wall. I began to slowly squeeze my trigger, sending a round to that exact spot of the corner of the building closest to the mob.

Concrete sprayed across the crowd.

The crowd began to disperse, running in all directions. The street was clear now. Mogadishu came to mind again. *We aren't going down like that today; no fucking way.*

I did my follow-through—keeping the trigger to the rear, I kept my sight alignment on the target, ensuring my round had hit exactly where I'd wanted it to—and then I closed my mouth and ground my teeth, feeling a sense of joy that my idea had actually worked. I'd removed the mob's threat against the convoy without killing a single person.

I looked over to the 10th Mountain lieutenant, who said, "Holy shit! Nice shot!"

"We've still got movement around those buildings and rooftops to our right, 300 meters away," I said, and he replied, "Roger." He walked over to the lead vehicle, to inform them of the enemy movement, and at that time the MK19 gunner swiveled around, facing northwest toward the rooftops.

Perhaps a minute passed and then all hell broke loose. AK-47s opened up from rooftops, alleys, and street corners, hammering us from all compass points. It was like a boxing match, I remember thinking, and we were going toe-to-toe with the enemy. For once in Iraq, the insurgents had decided to trade hooks and uppercuts with us.

We weren't moving and they weren't running away. Walls of fire were rolling in both directions, and 10th Mountain soldiers were yelling, "Where the hell is it coming from?" as they returned fire, scoping the rooftops. I knew we could not remain without the high ground for long, without becoming sitting ducks. A fundamental law of war: He who holds the high ground wins the fight.

We were surrounded by 7.62 caliber rounds, cracking by us, flying over us, and hitting the street. I took a low knee in the back of the Humvee, ducking down and then peeking up, zeroing in on muzzle flashes on the rooftops. I looked over at Martin and said, "Hey, Martin, we're getting fired at now!"

"No shit!" he shouted back, grinning with the little smirk he had whenever we were under fire.

I could see a yellow heavy-equipment crane, missing its tracks, about 100 meters northwest of us. *If I can get to that crane, I can set up and start taking out the enemy,* I thought, *so the infantry squads can advance to the dirt berm.* The berm was 50 meters west of the crane, in front of it. I knew that if I could get to the crane, 10th Mountain would follow; we'd be closer to the enemy, making it easier for us to strike and kill the insurgents.

I kept ducking and rising, trying to locate the enemy and get a better feel for potential cover near the crane. Nobody had advanced yet; nobody had moved toward the enemy. Luckily for us, the enemy couldn't shoot for shit, but their fire was still heavy over and around us, AK rounds pinging off Humvees and striking sand and rocks, dust trails zinging off the dirt road.

Make it to the crane, I thought, *make it to the crane.*

I knew it was risky, given that it was a 100-meter dash with no cover in between. You're never supposed to be up for more than three seconds when you're under fire. The saying goes, "I'm up, he sees me, I'm down." All American infantry are trained to rush for three seconds under fire, then roll or take cover, and then move again, in a pattern of three-second rushes, until you can find cover or you have reached the objective. This is also true for special operations. What a lot of people in combat tend to forget is that if you can see the enemy, the enemy can see you. Nobody's invincible. As bold as many of us think we are, the bottom line is that nobody is Superman in war.

But every so often you have to go for broke. Trusting your instincts means that sometimes, you have to take a real risk. The plain damn fact was, I knew that the crane would provide ideal cover to kill the enemy, and the only way to get there was to haul ass, hell for leather. For a split second, I remember telling myself, *Should've brought more water!*

I ducked down and yelled to Robi, "Stay here; stay behind cover."

In his usual low-key tone, he said, "Roger."

"Hey, Robi," I said, and he looked at me. "You want to see something crazy?" I looked at him, said "Watch this!" and leapt over the side of the Humvee with my rifle in my right hand and a small field radio tucked into my vest. I landed on both feet as the enemy fire increased, kicking up rounds in the dirt around me. I sprinted fast and hard, running first at about a 30-degree angle north and then aiming straight for the crane.

I could hear enemy fire all around me, and the shouts of 10th Mountain soldiers behind me. I remember thinking, *Damn, it's hot.* Soaked with sweat, I was closing in on the crane, Kalashnikov fire cracking next to me. I have never run faster in my life.

Somehow, by the grace of God, I made it. I got down behind the back side of the crane, breathing heavily, trying to catch my breath. I took one deep breath and let it out, trying to calm myself down. I got into the prone and crawled underneath the crane so that I'd have cover above me. As I was lying under the crane, I realized I didn't have good-enough elevation to engage the rooftops. Since the tracks were off the wheels of the crane, I wedged myself between the body and the top of the track—I was lying on the left wheel. Steel surrounded me. I could hear bullets hitting the crane, pinging and ricocheting in all directions.

Now I had a better line of sight to start engaging the enemy on the rooftops. I fired three rounds, rapidly, on semiautomatic, at an insurgent on a rooftop who was firing an AK-47. He disappeared with my last round. I don't know if I killed him, but right away, the fire stopped from that rooftop. I knew it was crucial now for 10th Mountain infantrymen to push up toward my position and begin engaging the enemy. Tenth Mountain was with my Ranger brothers in Mogadishu and they were with me now in Fallujah.

I grabbed my radio, called in my location at the crane, and told them that they were good, now, to push forward up to the dirt berm, roughly 50 meters in front of me.

"Roger," said the 10th Mountain RTO.

I don't know which RTO it was; it may have been Specialist Patrick Lybert, twenty-five, from Ladysmith, Wisconsin, who was killed in action on June 21, 2006, fighting against the Taliban in Afghanistan. (At the time of his death in Afghanistan, Lybert was a squad leader and a staff sergeant.)

I thought it would be best for me to stay put, and keep scanning for—and killing more—enemy. I stayed under the crane, snug between the wheel and the body, as enemy rounds continued slamming into the crane, thudding off the metal in an odd rhythm: first, a few would hit, equally spaced, followed by a barrage of bullets hitting the crane all at once. I said out loud to myself, "I'll stay here until I can hear 10th Mountain coming up, from the rear." Tenth Mountain knew that I was somewhere around the crane, but they didn't know exactly where I was, in my cover, within the crane. I heard them approaching, what seemed to be a squad of infantry. Before I knew it they had passed the crane, moving quickly to the dirt berm. Once they had pushed in front of me and were on the berm, I dropped my barrel down so that I wouldn't be pointing at their backs.

I located and grabbed my three expended brass because first, a sniper should never shoot more than three rounds from one position. And second, you should never leave brass in combat as a sniper, in order to prevent the enemy from counter-tracking you. I tucked the three expended brass into a small pocket I'd made on the left forearm sleeve of my blouse. I slipped out of my cover and got under the crane, then slid out backwards, keeping the crane between me and the enemy.

Coming out on one knee, I switched radio channels to the Scout frequency and called Martin. "Do you see the dirt berm at your two o'clock? Meet me there."

"Roger," he replied.

I tucked my radio away back on my vest now and hustled up, moving out quickly around the right side of the crane, heading up to the berm to the 10th Mountain squad. Strangely, the enemy fire had stopped for a moment. Then, just a few seconds later, fire came down on us again as soldiers were moving, taking cover, and trying to locate the insurgents. Enemy fire slowed to pop shots, and the 10th Mountain soldiers were carefully selecting targets, wisely conserving ammunition.

We had no idea, really, of what to expect, as happens all too often in combat. Turns out we were an hour into what proved to be a three-hour firefight.

As I ran up to the berm, I noticed there were 10th Mountain light infantrymen in the prone all across the berm. I realized I didn't want to be at either end of the squad, because that would make me stand out to the enemy. As a sniper, you always want to blend into your surroundings; in this case, it was an infantry squad, and I wanted to make myself as inconspicuous as possible—as if I was indeed one of them, a grunt with a rifle, returning fire.

I saw an opening on the right side of the squad, toward the end of their line of soldiers, and I set up next to a rifleman who was firing on single shot, engaging the enemy on the rooftops with his M4.

"Don't get too carried away; only shoot what you can hit," I said to him as I scoped the rooftops. The truth is, if you let an infantryman keep shooting, he will. Privates, especially, rarely think about conserving ammunition.

I did a quick scan of my surroundings and saw a gray concrete building in front of me and more buildings off to the left. There were minarets of mosques far off in the distance, toward downtown Fallujah, and I could see a paved road in the distance, running north-south. I knew the road was quite a fair stretch, but didn't know exactly how far away at that very moment. Everything was going down quickly, and I was anxious for Martin to show up and spot for me. Enemy fire was sporadic, at this point, and 10th Mountain soldiers continued to return fire.

More and more soldiers began to arrive and throw down on the enemy, slowly turning our hasty fighting position into a defensive perimeter. Within seconds, Martin arrived, out of breath and gasping, but on the case.

"You're a crazy motherfucker, you know that?"

"That's what I keep hearing," I replied.

I immediately pointed out the road to Martin and remember saying, "If anything comes our way, that road is going to be a key avenue of approach. That road needs to be our main focus."

Fallujah insurgents were using pickup trucks as gun platforms, which Al-Qaeda and Somali rebels in Mogadishu had done in 1993, and which we'd been briefed on in Iraq, on many occasions. We were all aware of the fact that insurgents and terrorists in Iraq often mounted heavy machine guns on pickup trucks, thus turning them into gun trucks.

Martin agreed, shouting to a 10th Mountain platoon leader, "Hey, sir, be aware of that road!" Martin turned back around now, staring at the road, his eyes fixed on a far distant point perhaps 800 meters away.

I said to him, "Some leaders' recon," thinking that you're never supposed to make contact on any kind of reconnaissance, and of course, we had most definitely made contact and remained engaged.

He smirked and replied, "No shit, huh."

Enemy fire kept rolling, the rounds kicking up dust and sand around us and 10th Mountain. My main concern now was the road, and my intent was to do everything possible as a sniper to keep the enemy from advancing on us, using that road to kill us and 10th Mountain. I remained the only sniper on the ground, with 10th Mountain, at this point. Because this was supposed to be a leaders' recon, no other snipers had been attached to 10th Mountain on this day. Moreover, because this was a leaders' recon, we had no spotting scope or any binoculars to see past my Leupold 10x fixed scope on my SR-25. Fortunately, my Leupold was solid, and with it, I could see out to 1,500 meters; at 200 meters, I could see someone's eyelashes. But we had no spotting scope, which I remembered thinking would be a key lesson learned, if we survived that day.

Martin only had an ACOG 4x32 scope, a normal scope on his M4. You can see out to 800 meters through that scope, and it has tritium to illuminate its reticules at night. There was a saying for the Ranger battalion, when new equipment like the ACOG would come out in the army in the late 1990s: "Give it to the Rangers; if they can't break it, it's good." We Rangers were known for destroying an objective to the point where there was nothing left standing, and for testing new equipment to its maximum durability.

In the prone, looking through my scope, I said to Martin, "We need to figure out a distance to that road, so I can start putting my dope together in case I need to take a shot."

Martin, of course, was also a sniper team leader; in that way, it was quite fortunate he was my "Johnny on the Spot" acting, ad hoc spotter, because we'd both graduated from the U.S. Army Sniper School at Fort Benning.

Without spotting scope and binoculars, I had to rely solely on my range-estimation training from Sniper School. I knew, off the top of my head, that in open, flat desert terrain, you tend to underestimate your target distance. I factored that in and "guesstimated" the distance to the road.

A strange quiet descended all around us, and the 10th Mountain soldiers on the berm began changing magazines and drinking water. Everyone's uniform was dark with sweat and we were all red-faced and baked from the desert sun. The chain of command was rocking: Fire team leaders were checking rounds and water on each soldier and the light machine gunners were reporting to their fire team leaders, who then reported up to their squad leaders. You could hear grunts saying, "Fuck these insurgent motherfuckers!"

Staying in the prone, and figuring out the distance to the road, I heard from my left, "LeBleu!" I picked up my sniper rifle and sprinted over, peeling off left from the berm and hustling over toward my seven o'clock. I took a knee next to a 10th Mountain soldier firing an M4/M203. I nodded to him and he nodded back, sucking water from a hose connected to the Camel Bak water pouch on his back. He looked kind of wiped out, but his eyes were hard; he still had a lot of fight in him.

Kneeling, I began scanning from south to west, looking over the desert and mud huts far on the horizon. As I was scoping the desert, the soldier eyed the scope on his M4, leaning forward, looking south.

"There's a guy on a red motorcycle coming up the road," he said excitedly, all in one breath.

"That's the fuckin' triggerman for the IED," I said.

I knew that previous IED ambushes in Fallujah had been set off by one or two men on motorcycles. Turning right, I scoped the road and could see the man on the red motorcycle, with a red *khaffiyeh* wrapped turban-style around his head, wearing a white *dishdasha*, otherwise known as a "man dress." I was looking closely at him, searching for a cell phone, a weapon or a package—anything out of the ordinary.

He was about 75 meters away, approaching the crowd west of us, and at that moment, I thought, *He's more than likely headed into Fallujah.* I told the 10th Mountain soldier, "He's got nothing on him," and then I heard my name shouted from the berm. I could tell it was Martin. I sprang up and sprinted back to the berm. As I approached, someone from 10th Mountain began shouting, "That's the white truck—that's the fuckin' white truck!"

I realized in the middle of running back to the berm that it was no doubt the same white pickup truck we'd seen at the beginning of the IED ambush. As I dashed over to Martin, I was already preparing myself for a shot, thinking of range and the wind—I was damn glad that there was no wind that day. I hit the berm on my left shoulder and rolled over sideways, kind of submarining myself into the dirt berm—not exactly in the prone and certainly, not in the solid, correct firing position that I would've liked to line up a long-range shot. Sweat burned down my face.

I set my elevation to 800 meters on my Leupold scope, thinking that if need be, I could use Kentucky windage to line up the shot. There was no time to get into a better firing position. I could see the truck now through my scope, traveling from south to north, at what I guessed to be between 20 and 25 miles an hour. I could see that he was headed toward a factory located at least a mile north of his position, in the Boneyard. I knew that once he got inside the factory grounds, not only would I lose the shot, but it was also likely he'd grab more insurgents and load up the bed of that pickup with more AK-47s, and perhaps a heavy machine gun and RPGs.

Looking through my scope, I could see four insurgents with AK-47s held between their legs in the bed of the pickup, and a driver and passenger up front. I had chosen as my target an insurgent who was standing all the way up in the back of the truck, a big, broad-shouldered man. He was leaning forward slightly against the cab, a curved banana clip jammed in the AK, the wooden stock of the Kalashnikov up against his right shoulder, ready to fire. Ideally, you want to take out the wheelman, stopping the vehicle all together, if not causing an accident. Unfortunately, I didn't have that option available to me.

While I was tracking the white pickup, I said to Martin, "Act as my spotter on this."

"Yeah, I got you."

Martin looked through his ACOG on his M4. I gave him my reading and elevation setting, all at once, saying, "Eight hundred, no wind."

"Okay."

At that second, a 10th Mountain platoon leader shouted, "Does anyone have a shot on that white truck?"

I realized that not only did I have the shot, but I was also the only person on the berm with a weapon that could reach the white pickup truck. The light machine guns on the berm, known as M249 SAWs (Squad Automatic Weapons), could reach 800 meters, but had proven in combat in Iraq to be much more effective up to 600 meters.

I yelled out, "I've got it," and I heard, "Take the shot."

That's all I needed to hear.

I was tracking the white pickup truck the whole time and could see the sun reflecting off the barrels of their Kalashnikovs. The driver was wearing a white *dishdasha* and a grayish-white turban. The passenger wore a dark blouse with no *khaffiyeh*. He had short, greasy black hair. He looked fairly young, perhaps in his late teens. Two insurgents were squatting down in the bed of the pickup, near the tailgate. They wore dark *dishdashas* and their barrels were sticking straight up from between their legs.

Bore-sighted now, I could see sunlight gleaming off their muzzles. My target was clad in a dark shirt and gray trousers, and also wore no headdress. He had his right hand on the trigger of his AK, the Kalashnikov still shouldered, at the ready. I could see the wavy, dark grains in the wood of his stock. To his left, an insurgent was in a black *dishdasha*, his AK now disappeared within his man dress, his left hand jammed into his body. I remember thinking, *None of them are wearing headdresses,* filing that fact away into my dope for Fallujah, a key bit of field intelligence.

I knew that with the pickup moving at roughly 20 to 25 miles per hour, I'd have to give significant lead on the shot. I led it by one mil dot, which is more than your average lead in combat.

"Give it daylight," Martin said calmly, which is shorthand in sniper language, meaning, "Give it enough lead, lead the target." I took a very quick relaxation breath, because I was still breathing hard from the mad dash back to the berm, and feeling very rushed, I said quickly to Martin, "Taking the shot."

"Send it," Martin replied.

With my index finger on the trigger, the metal touching the meaty portion between the tip and first bone joint, I slowly but steadily pulled the trigger to the rear. Conscious of my breathing and exhaling slowly, I pulled the trigger, sending my first round toward the pickup. *Round fired.* I saw dirt kick up just before the road, and I realized I was quite short. The white pickup rolled on, not changing speed; no one in the bed of the pickup even looked at the spot where my round had hit the sand.

At least 200 meters short, I reckoned, watching the dust fall from the short round.

Martin said, "Short, right in front of the road."

I replied, "Roger."

Holy shit, how far away is this? I thought. I knew that it was considerably more than 800 meters now. The pickup truck was easily halfway to the looted factory in the Boneyard, insurgents in the back, their rifles held close to them. I was still zeroed in; I'd never taken my eye off the glass. My target continued to keep his Kalashnikov shouldered.

At that time, without looking, I reached up with my left hand to the elevation knob on my scope. I never took my eyes off my target, and still tracking the pickup, I twisted the knob a quarter turn.

Martin said, "One thousand meters."

"Sending second shot," I replied, keeping my right index finger on the trigger.

"Send it."

Taking in a quick breath, I started to exhale. Very slowly now, I applied pressure to the trigger, pulling it back, and I sent my second shot. I kept my follow-through, holding my trigger to the rear now, following the pickup through the scope. I saw the round hit the insurgent below the stock of his rifle, about midsection, on his right side. He dropped and fell backwards into the bed of the pickup, his Kalashnikov falling into the road.

"Hit," Martin replied in a conversational tone, calm and professional.

A 10th Mountain RTO to Martin's right shouted, "Holy shit, you got him! Fuckin' A!"

I didn't even know that the RTO was there. I reckon he'd been watching the entire action through his scope, during which only about five to six seconds had passed, even though it seemed much longer. Combat is strange that way; the smallest moments can turn into slow motion. There was a silence over all of us and then, we were taking fire again. Drop of a hat, it all went dead quiet.

Watching the white pickup through my scope, it seemed I'd surprised the other three insurgents in the back, as if I wasn't supposed to be able to reach them with one round from an American sniper rifle. As the American infantry proverb states, "One well-aimed round can change the course of combat." By now I could tell that the insurgents in the white pickup were surprised as hell. The two guys in the back, near the tailgate, dropped their AKs, as the third guy in the bed of the pickup quickly turned around and dove down. The pickup came to a screeching halt, dust kicking up all around it. They threw the dead insurgent over the driver's side onto the ground, where a pool of blood quickly formed.

The two remaining insurgents—carrying AK-47s and dressed in dark gray and black *dishdashas* but wearing no ninja-style *khaffiyehs*—ran out of an alley and jumped into the bed of the pickup. I remember thinking of the fallen insurgent, *Is he really dead, or is he going to get up and run?* I kept eyeing his body through my scope. Everything was moving so fast now. I looked hard at his body to see if his chest was rising and falling, but it was motionless. After a few seconds had passed, it was clear to me that he was dead. At that same moment, the pickup hightailed it toward the factory.

"The pickup truck is speeding off," I said to Martin as I continued looking through my scope. Martin yelled back to 10th Mountain, "We got a hit, but two more guys jumped in the bed." The truck rolled hard, blowing past the factory, a huge cloud of dust following behind as it disappeared south. *Why the hell didn't 10th Mountain turn loose our .50 cal and MK19 on the pickup, right after I killed the insurgent?* Why did they let it get away? I'd marked the target. They had the range. This reflected a severe problem with our rules of engagement in the Iraq War, beyond May 1, 2003: Our grunts were being conditioned to fire only if fired upon first—giving battlefield initiative away to insurgents and terrorists—even though our rules of engagement clearly stated that when you see anyone carrying an AK-47 or any other weapon of war, deadly force is authorized.

The reality on the ground, however, was that once straight-up combat rules of engagement were rescinded by the Bush administration in May 2003, Department of Defense lawyers were all over Iraq, investigating grunts who were throwing down on insurgents and terrorists. Our infantrymen knew their careers were on the line anytime they pulled the trigger—which is not what you want a warrior thinking in the heat of battle.

Since no one in the white pickup truck had fired on 10th Mountain, our grunts hadn't fired back. As I lay there, in the prone, staying bore-sighted, I regretted this change in the rules of engagement. A well-known law of war says that once a sniper has marked an enemy vehicle—such as the white pickup carrying insurgents with AK-47s—all supporting heavy guns should light it up and destroy it. I made a mental note for my field Intel: *Remind grunts to kill the enemy once a sniper marks a target.*

Two women came out and dragged the body of the dead insurgent away, which happened quite often at war in Iraq—people always came out of nowhere and picked up dead insurgents. I would always refer to this phenomenon as "fighting ghosts," because the bodies were never left lying around. I assumed it was due to religious reasons, but it was extremely different and new to me. I was pissed off, thinking, "That was my kill, and they are taking it away from me!"

I glanced up to look at my elevation. It read 1,100 meters. *Holy shit, that was a long shot!*

I said to Martin, "That was eleven hundred meters."

"No shit," Martin said calmly.

I kept saying to myself, *I just got an eleven-hundred-meter confirmed kill, on a moving target,* over and over again, somewhat amazed that I'd made the shot.

"Good thing there was no wind," I said.

"Yep," Martin said, still looking through his spotting scope.

Martin came off his scope now, smiling at me, and said, "You lucky fucker."

CHAPTER SEVEN

The Sniper in the Trenches

Major H. Hesketh-Prichard

SNIPING, WHICH IS TO BE DEFINED IN A BROAD WAY AS THE ART OF VERY accurate shooting from concealment or in the open, did not exist as an organized thing at the beginning of the war. The wonderful rapid fire which was the glory of the original expeditionary force was not sniping, nor was it, beyond a certain degree, accurate. Its aim was to create a "beaten zone" through which nothing living could pass; and this business was not best served by very accurate individual shooting. Rather it was served by rapid fire under skilled fire-control.

But when we settled down to trench warfare, and the most skillful might spend a month in the trenches without ever seeing, except perhaps at dawn, the whole of a German, and when during the day one got but a glimpse or two of the troglodytic enemy, there arose this need for very accurate shooting. The mark was often but a head or half a face, or a loophole behind which lurked a German sniper, and no sighting shot was possible because it "put down the target." The smallest of big game animals did not present so small a mark as the German head, so that sniping became the highest and most difficult of all forms of rifle shooting. At it, every good target shot, though always useful, was not necessarily successful, for speed was only less necessary than accuracy, and no sniper could be considered worthy of the name who could not get off his shot within two seconds of sighting his target.

So much for the sniper in trench warfare, of which a certain clique in the Army held him to be the product. The officers who believed this prophesied that when warfare became once more open, he would be useless. This proved perhaps one of the most shortsighted views of the whole war, for when it became our turn to attack, the sniper's duties only broadened out. Should a battalion take a trench, it was the duty of snipers to lie out in front and keep down the German heads during the consolidation of their newly-won position by our men, and were we held up by a machine-gun in advance, it was often the duty of a couple of snipers to crawl forward and, if possible, deal with the obstruction.

The sniper is not, and from the first, as I saw him, *never was meant to be, a product of trench warfare*. In modern war, where a battalion may be held up by a machine-gun, it is invaluable to have in that battalion a number of picked shots who can knock that machine-gun out. For this purpose in some of our later attacks a sniper carried armour-piercing ammunition, and did not shoot at the machine-gunners, but at the machine-gun itself. A single hit on the casing of the breech-block, and the machine-gun was rendered useless.

In the Army there has always been in certain quarters a prejudice against very accurate shooting, a prejudice which is quite understandable when one considers the aims and ends of musketry. While sniping is the opportunism of the rifle, musketry is its routine. It would obviously never do to diminish the depth of your beaten zone by excess of accuracy. But this war, which, whatever may be said to the contrary—and much was said to the contrary—was largely a war of specialists, changed many things, and among them the accurate shot or sniper was destined to prove his extraordinary value.

But a great deal that I have said in the foregoing paragraphs only became clear later, and at the moment of which I am writing, September and October, 1915, the superiority lay with the Germans, and the one problem was to defeat them at a game which they had themselves started. For it was the Germans, and not the British, who began sniping.

That the Germans were ready for a sniping campaign is clear enough, for at the end of 1914 there were already 20,000 telescopic sights in the German Army, and their snipers had been trained to use them. To make any accurate estimate of how many victims the Hun snipers claimed at this period is naturally impossible, but the blow which they struck for their side was a heavy one, and many of our finest soldiers met their deaths at their hands. In the struggle which followed there was perhaps something more human and more personal than in the work of the gunner or the infantryman. The British or Colonial sniper was pitted against the Bavarian or the Prussian, and all along the front duels were fought between men who usually saw no more of their antagonists than a cap badge or a forehead, but who became personalities to each other, with names and individualities.

Only the man who actually was a sniper in the trenches in 1915 can know how hard the German was to overcome. At the end of 1914 there were, as I have said, 20,000 telescopic sights in the German Army, and the Duke of Ratibor did good work for the Fatherland when he collected all the sporting rifles in Germany (and there were thousands of them) and sent them to the Western front, which was already well equipped with the military issue.

Armed with these the German snipers were able to make wonderfully fine shooting. Against them, lacking as we did a proper issue of telescopic-sighted rifles, we had to pit only the blunt open sights of the service rifle, except here and there where the deer stalkers of Scotland (who possessed such weapons) lent their Mannlichers and their Mausers. But for these there was no great supply of ammunition, and many had to be returned to their cases for this reason.

At this time the skill of the German sniper had become a by-word, and in the early days of trench warfare brave German riflemen used to lie out between the lines, sending their bullets through the head of any officer or man who dared to look over our parapet. These Germans, who were often Forest Guards, and sometimes Battle Police, did their business with a skill and a gallantry which must be very freely acknowledged. From the ruined house or the field of decaying roots, sometimes resting their rifles on the bodies of the dead, they sent forth a plague of head-wounds into the British lines. Their marks were small, but when they hit they usually killed their man, and the hardiest soldier turned sick when he saw the effect of the pointed German bullet, which was apt to keyhole so that the little hole in the forehead where it entered often became a huge tear, the size of a man's fist, on the other side of the stricken man's head. That occasional snipers on the Hun side reversed their bullets, thus making them into dum-dums, is incontrovertible, because we were continually capturing clips of such bullets, but it must also be remembered that many bullets keyholed which were not so reversed. Throughout the war I saw thousands of our snipers' bullets, and I never saw one which had been filed away or otherwise treated with a view to its expanding upon impact.

At that time in the German Army there was a system of roving snipers; that is, a sniper was given a certain stretch of trench to patrol, usually about half a mile, and it was the duty of sentries along his beat to find and point out targets for him. This information I got from a prisoner whom I examined soon after I went down to the trenches. Indeed, I used to go any distance to get the chance of examining a prisoner and so learn something of the German organization.

One deserter gave quite a lot of information. He had the Iron Cross, and was a sergeant. One of the scenes that always remains with me is the examination of this man on a rainy, foggy night by the light of a flaring smoky lamp in the room of an *estaminet* just behind the lines. As time went on it became very difficult for a German prisoner to lead me astray with wrong information. There were so many questions to which one got to know the answers, and which must be more or less common knowledge to German riflemen.

The demeanour of prisoners was very diverse. Some would give no answers—brave fellows these, whom we respected; others would volunteer a good deal of false statement; others yet again were so eager to answer all questions that when they did not know they made a guess. But one way and another, through them all I gained an immense amount of information as to the German sniping organization.

It would appear that the telescopic-sighted rifles in the German army were served out in the ratio of six per company, and that these rifles were issued not to the private soldiers who shot with them, but to N.C.O.'s who were responsible for their accuracy, and from whom the actual privates who used the rifles obtained them, handing them back at given intervals for inspection. In the top of the case of each German telescopic sight were quite short and very clear instructions, a very different matter to the conditions obtaining upon our side, where very often, as I have before stated, the man using the telescopic sight knew nothing about it.

On one occasion I had gone down on duty to a certain stretch of trench and there found a puzzled-looking private with a beautiful new rifle fitted with an Evans telescopic sight.

"That is a nice sight," said I.

"Yessir."

I examined the elevating drum, and saw that it was set for one hundred yards.

"Look here," I said, "you have got the sight set for a hundred. The Hun trenches are four hundred yards away."

The private looked puzzled.

"Have you ever shot with that rifle?" I asked.

"No, sir."

"Do you understand it?"

"No, sir."

"How did you get it?"

"It was issued to me as trench stores, sir."

"Who by?"

"The Quartermaster Sergeant, sir."

Certainly many a German owed his life in those earlier days to the fact that so many of the telescopic-sighted rifles in the British Expeditionary Force were incorrectly sighted to the hold of the men using them. By this I mean that some men hold tightly and some men hold loosely, and there may be a difference at a hundred yards of six inches in the shooting of the same rifle in different hands. To hand over the rifle as "trench stores," in which case it would be shot by different men of different battalions, was simply to do away with the accuracy which formed its only asset.

But to return to the examination of German prisoners. One point cropped up over and over again, and this was the ease with which German snipers quite frankly owned that they were able to distinguish between our officers and men in an attack because, as one said naively: "the legs of the officers are thinner than the legs of the men." There are hundreds and hundreds of our officers lying dead in France and Flanders whose death was solely due to the cut of their riding breeches. It is no use wearing a Tommy's tunic and a webbing belt, if the tell-tale riding trousers are not replaced by more commonplace garments.

In 1915 there were very few loopholes in the British trenches, whereas the Germans had a magnificent system. In early days when I used to be told at Brigade Headquarters that there was a German sniper at such and such a map reference, and I was to go and try to put him out of action, I very rarely found a loophole from which I could reconnoitre him, and as every German sniper seemed to be supported on either flank by other German snipers, looking for him with one's head over the top of the parapet was, if made a continual practice, simply a form of suicide. I used, therefore, to have a couple of sandbags filled with stones and rubble placed as inconspicuously as possible on the top of the parapet. No ball will pierce a sandbag full of stones, and it was thus that one got the opportunity of a good look at the German trenches without fear of receiving a bullet from either flank.

At this time the efforts to camouflage our loopholes were extraordinarily primitive—indeed, concealment was nearly impossible in the form of parapet then in use. Many of our units took an actual pride in having an absolutely flat and even parapet, which gave the Germans every opportunity of spotting the smallest movement. The parapets were made of sandbags beaten down with spades, and it is not too much to say that along many of them a mouse could not move without being observed by the most moderate-sighted German sniper. It was curious how some few commanding officers stuck to these flat parapets in the face of all casualties and the dictates of common-sense, even after the High Command had issued orders upon the subject. At a later date a trial was instituted, and proved that in spotting and shooting at a dummy head exposed for two and four seconds over a flat parapet, the number of hits was three to one, as compared with the same exposure when made over an imitation German parapet.

Over on the other side of No Man's Land the German trenches presented a quite different appearance from ours—ours being beaten down, as I have said, until they made as clear a line as a breakwater. The German trenches were deeper, with much more wire in front, and from our point of view looked like the course of a gigantic mole which had flung up uneven heaps of earth. Here and there, a huge piece of corrugated iron would be flung upon the parapet, and pinned there with a stake. Here and there stood one of those steel boxes, more or less well concealed under a heap of earth, from which set rifles fired all night. Here and there lay great piles of sandbags, black, red, green, striped, blue, dazzling our eyes. It was said that the Germans used the pink and red ones to look round, because they approximated to flesh colour, but this was no doubt apocryphal. But what was not apocryphal was the fact that the Germans had a splendid parapet behind which a man could move and over which he could look with comparative impunity, whereas we in this respect gave heavy hostages to fortune.

There was one protection which was always sound, and which could be put into immediate operation, and that was to teach our men to hang as many rags as possible upon our wire, and wherever else they could in the region of our parapet. These fluttering rags continually caught the German eyes, which were drawn by the movement of the rags in the wind. It is possible that, if the truth were recognized, those simple little rags saved many a life during the course of the war. Of course, there were battalions in which attempts had been made to remedy these defects, as there was one type of officer whom one occasionally came across. This was the soldier who had done a certain amount of stalking, or big-game shooting, and it is not too much to say that wherever there was such an officer, there were usually two or three extra telescopes and telescopic-sighted rifles, and various well-concealed posts from which to use them.

The Intelligence report, which was each day forwarded to Brigade, was also full and accurate. Indeed, the truth of the matter forced itself upon me, as I spent day after day in the trenches. *What was wanted, apart from organization, was neither more nor less than the hunter spirit.* The hunter spends his life in trying to outwit some difficult quarry, and the step between war and hunting is but a very small one. It is inconceivable that a skilled hunter in a position of command should ever allow his men to suffer as our men sometimes did in France. It was all so simple and so obvious. The Canadian Division and, later, the Canadian Corps was full of officers who understood how to deal with the German sniper, and early in the war there were Canadian snipers who were told off to this duty, and some of them were extraordinarily successful. Corporal, afterwards Lieutenant, Christie, of the P.P.C.L.I., was one of the individual pioneers of sniping. He had spent his life hunting in the Yukon, and he simply turned the same qualities which had brought him within the range of the mountain sheep to the downfall of Fritz the Forest Guard.

In the long monotony of the trenches during that bleak winter of 1915, the only respite besides work which was possible to our soldiers was the element of sport and excitement introduced by sniping and its more important and elder sister, observation. Sniping in a dangerous sector—and there were many of these—was really neither more nor less than a very high-class form of big game shooting, in which the quarry shot back. As to danger, there are in Africa the lion, the elephant, the buffalo and the rhinoceros, and though the consensus of instructed opinion agrees that in proportion more hunters come back feet foremost from lion hunting than from the pursuit of the three other forms of dangerous game, yet I suppose that no one would dispute that the German sniper, especially when he is supported on either flank by *Kamaraden*, was far more dangerous in the long run than any lion.

In sniping, as the movement grew and sections were formed, one relied to an enormous extent upon the skill of the section to which the individual sniper belonged. A really first-rate man in a bad section was thrown away. First-rate men under a moderate officer were thrown away, and, worse than all, a good section under a good officer, who were relieved by the slack and poor section of another battalion, often suffered heavy casualties through no fault of their own.

Thus, the Royal Blankshires, who have an excellent sniping organization, build half a dozen skillfully hidden posts for observation and sniping purposes.

All kinds of precautions, which have become second nature, are taken to prevent these posts being given away to the enemy. The telescopes used are carefully wrapped in sandbags, their sunshades carefully extended lest the sun should, by flashing its reflection upon the object glass, give away the position. The loopholes in dry weather are damped before being fired through, and, most important of all, no one but the C.O., the sniping officer, and the snipers and observers are allowed in the posts. If anyone else enters them there are for him heavy penalties, which are always enforced. The result is that the Blankshires have a good tour of duty, lose no casualties to enemy snipers, and get splendid detail for their Intelligence reports.

They are relieved, however, by the Loamshires. The C.O. of this Battalion does not believe very much in sniping. He has a way of saying that sniping will "never win the war." He has, it is true, a sniping section because, and only because, his Brigadier and his Divisional General are keen about sniping, and continually come into the trenches and inquire about it. But the Loamshire sniping section is a pitiable affair. They take over from the Royal Blanks.

"These are jolly good observation posts," says the Royal Blanks sniping officer. He is the real thing, and he dreams of his job in the night. "But one has to be a bit careful not to give them away. I never let my fellows use the one in Sap F until the sun has worked round behind us."

"Aw—right oh!" says the Loamshire opposite number.

"One has to be a bit careful about the curtains at the back of those loopholes in Perrier Alley. The light's apt to shine through."

"Aw—right oh!" says the Loamshire officer.

"We are leaving our range-cards."

"Aw—right oh!"

So the keen Royal Blanks officer and his keen section go out into rest billets, and do not visit the trenches again till they come back to take over from the Loamshires.

"Well, how are the posts?" asks the Royal Blanks officer, cheerily.

"Pretty rotten; they were all busted up the first day."

"Damn! They took us a fortnight to build."

"Well, they are busted up all right."

"Did your fellows give them away, do you think?"

"Oh, no!"

Now, as a matter of fact, the moment the Royal Blankshires were out of the trenches the Loamshire snipers, who knew no better, had used the

O.P.s for promiscuous firing, and the posts which had been so jealously guarded under the Blankshire regime had been invaded by Loamshire officers and men in need of a view of the German trenches—or of sleep. The curtains that kept the loopholes dark had been turned back. The result was as might have been expected. The watching German, who had suffered from those posts without being able to locate them when the Blankshires were in the trenches, now spotted them, rang up their guns, and had them demolished, not without casualties to the Loamshires. So the work was all to be done again—but no sooner does the keen Blankshire officer build up a post than the slack Loamshire officer allows it to be given away. It is now a case for the Royal Blanks C.O. to take up with the Loamshire C.O.

Such were the difficulties of the keen officer when the opposite number of the relieving battalion was a "dud."

Conscientiousness is a great quality in an officer, but in the Sniping, Scouting and Observation Officer something more was needed. To obtain success, real success, it was necessary that his should be a labour of love. He must think and dream of his work at all hours and all times, and it was wonderful how many came to do this. In the battalion the Intelligence and Sniping officer had always a sporting job, and if he suffered in promotion (as do nearly all specialists in any great Army) yet he had the compensations which come to an artist in love with his work.

There were at this time one or two other factors in the situation to which I must allude in order that the reader may understand the position as it was then. The enemy had an immense preponderance in trench weapons such as *minenwerfer*. The result was that a too successful bout of British sniping sometimes drew a bombardment. The activity of snipers was therefore not always welcome to short-sighted officers, who distinctly and naturally objected to the enemy riflemen calling in the assistance of the parapet-destroying engines of war, in which they so outclassed us.

Soon, however, it was realized that the state of things obtaining while the German held the mastery of aimed rifle-fire could not be permitted to continue—the casualties were too great—and I will now give some account of the instruction and experience in the trenches that went on while we were attempting to capture the sniping initiative from the enemy.

Towards the end of October, 1915, I was ordered to report to the 48th Division, then holding a line in the neighbourhood of Hebuterne. I was to proceed to Divisional Headquarters behind Pas, and was there ordered to Authie, where a number of officers were to come for instruction. This instruction was, as usual, to be divided between the back areas and the front line. I had applied for the services of my friend, Lieut. G. M. Gathorne-Hardy, an experienced shot, and skilled user of the telescope, who had been on many shooting trips in different parts of the world with me and others. At Authie we at once settled down to work; the officers going through a course which need not be detailed here. Suffice it to say that the telescopic-sighted rifles of all the battalions in the Division were shot and corrected, and various plans which we had formed for the destruction of German snipers were rehearsed.

On the third day arrangements were made by Division as to which trenches we were to visit, and after duly reporting at Brigade Headquarters in a dug-out in Hebuterne, we proceeded upon our way.

It is not an easy thing to instruct five or six officers in the line in sniping—the number is too large—so as soon as we entered the trenches I divided my class into three parties, and assigned to each an area in which to look for German snipers, Gathorne-Hardy and I going from one group to another.

At the point at which we entered the front line trenches, our line was a little higher than that of the enemy, so that the initial advantage was certainly with us, and almost at once G. (for so I shall refer to Capt. Gathorne-Hardy) spotted a German sniper who was just showing the top of his cap at the end of a sap. He was about three hundred and fifty or four hundred yards away, and though we watched him for half an hour, he gave no target. So we moved on. Examining the enemy line was enthralling work, as he had, even at that time, begun his campaign of skilled concealment, and was apt to set periscopes in trees, and steel boxes in all sorts of positions.

To spot and actually place these upon the map was as important a duty of the sniper as killing the enemy by rifle fire. For, once discovered, such strong points and emplacements could be dealt with by our artillery.

But to return. G. and I, after visiting the sections, acted together as shooter and observer. After spending a couple of hours examining the enemy line, we got into a disused trench and crawled back to a little bit of high ground from which we were able to overlook a group of poplar trees which grew between the lines, and which were said to be the haunt of a very capable German sniper.

Nothing, however, was to be seen of him, though we could clearly make out the nest he had built in one of the trees and, on the ground, what appeared to be either a dead man lying in the long grass or a tunic.

While we were here a message came down to say that No. 1 group had seen a party of nine Germans, and had wounded one of them. No. 2 party had not been successful.

At the time of which I write the Germans were just beginning to be a little shy of our snipers on those fronts to which organization had penetrated, and it was clear that the time would arrive when careful Hans and conscientious Fritz would become very troglodytic, as indeed they did. We had, therefore, turned our minds to think out plans and ruses by which the enemy might be persuaded to give us a target. We had noticed the extraordinary instinct of the German Officer to move to a flank, and thinking something might be made out of this, we collected all our officers and went back to the place where G. and I had spotted the Hun sniper or sentry at the end of the sap. A glance showed that he was still there.

I then explained my plan, which was that I should shoot at this sentry and in doing so, deliberately give away my position and rather act the tenderfoot, in the hope that some German officer would take a hand in the game and attempt to read me a lesson in tactics.

On either flank about 150 yards or so down the trench I placed the officers under instruction with telescopes and telescopic-sighted rifles, explaining to them that the enemy snipers would very possibly make an attempt to shoot at me from about opposite them. I then scattered a lot of dust in the loophole from which I intended to fire, and used a large .350 Mauser, which gave a good flash and smoke.

"Not yet."

"Now!"

"Telescopic sights, nurse your target."

As the sentry in the sap was showing an inch or two of his forehead as well as the peak of his cap, I had a very careful shot at him, which G., who was spotting for me with the glass, said went about twelve inches too high.

The sentry, of course, disappeared, and I at once poured in the whole magazine at a loophole plate, making it ring again, and by the dust and smoke handsomely giving away my own position. I waited a few minutes, and then commenced shooting again. Evidently my first essay had attracted attention, for two German snipers at once began firing at me from the right flank. At these two I fired back; they were almost exactly opposite the party under instruction, and it was clear that, if the party held their fire, the Germans would probably give fine targets. As a matter of fact, all that we hoped for actually happened, for the exasperated German snipers, thinking they had to deal only with a very great fool, began to fire over the parapet, their operations being directed by an officer with an immense pair of field-glasses. At the psychological moment, my officers opened fire, the large field-glasses dropped on the *wrong* side of the parapet, as the officer was shot through the head, and the snipers, who had increased to five or six, disappeared with complete suddenness. Nor did the enemy fire another shot.

It should be borne in mind, in reading the above, how great a plague were the skilled German snipers to us. One of them might easily cause thirty or forty casualties. Later in the war we had, on our side, many a sniper who killed his fifty or even his hundred of the enemy. Besides, as I have pointed out, in these early days of trench warfare the continual attrition caused by German snipers was very bad for *morale*.

At a later date we found a means by which we were able at once to find the position of any German sniper. For this purpose we used a dummy head made of papier-mâché.

The method of using was as follows: When a German sniper was giving trouble, we selected a good place opposite to him, and drove two stakes into our own parapet until only about a foot of them remained uncovered. To these we nailed a board on which was fashioned a groove which exactly fitted the stick or handle attached to the dummy head. This stick was inserted in the groove and the dummy head slowly pushed up above our parapet.

If the enemy sniper fired at and hit the head, the entry and exit of the bullet made two holes, one in the front, and one in the back of the hollow dummy head. The head, immediately on the shot, was pulled down by whoever was working it in as natural a manner as possible. The stick on which it was mounted was then replaced in the groove, but *exactly the height between the two glasses of a periscope lower* than the position in which it was when shot through.

Now all that remained to do was to place the lower glass of the periscope opposite the front hole in the head, and apply the eye to the rear hole and look into the periscope, the upper glass of which was above the parapet.

In this way we found ourselves looking along the path of the bullet, only in the opposite direction to that in which it had come, and, in the optical centre of the two holes, would be seen the German sniper who had fired the shot, or the post which concealed him. Once found he was soon dealt with. In trials at First Army Sniping School, we were able by this invention to locate sixty-seven snipers out of seventy-one.

Some of those who wanted to give the dummy head a specially lifelike appearance, placed a cigarette in its mouth, and smoked it through a rubber tube. It is a curious sensation to have the head through which you are smoking a cigarette suddenly shot with a Mauser bullet, but it is one that several snipers have experienced. After the incidents last described, we went up towards the flank, where the 4th Division lay alongside the 48th. It was in this Division that the 2nd Seaforth Highlanders had just played a delightful trick on the enemy. Someone in the battalion had obtained a mechanical stop, one of those ticking bits of mechanism which are made with a view to saving the employment of a human "stop" at covert-shoots. This particular stop was guaranteed to tick loudly for hours.

The Seaforths were facing the Germans across a very wild piece of No Man's Land. One night some adventurous and humorous spirit crawled out and placed the "stop" about sixty yards from the German parapet, and then set it going. The Germans at once leaped to the conclusion that the tick-tick-tick was the voice of some infernal machine, which would, in due time, explode and demolish them. They threw bombs, and fired flares, and officers and men spent a most haggard and horrible night, while opposite them the Scotsmen were laughing sardonically in their trenches. The whole incident was intensely typical of the careless and grim humour with which the Scottish regiments were at times apt to regard the Hun.

Another battalion at a much later date, when the Germans had become very shy, and mostly spent their off-duty hours in deep dug-outs, had the brilliant idea of preparing a notice board on which was printed in large letters and German: "Bitter Fighting in Berlin," and then, in smaller type, some apocryphal information. This notice it was their plan to raise, having first posted their snipers, who would be sure to obtain shots at the Huns who attempted to read the smaller lettering with their field-glasses. I do not think, however, that this plan was ever actually carried out. This was fortunate, since, though ingenious, the idea was not sound, as it would inevitably have led to a heavy bombardment of the trenches in which the notice was shown, and the game would not have been worth the candle.

To continue, however, with our day. Late in the afternoon, no Germans having shown themselves since the shooting of the officer—a heavy bombardment broke out on the right flank, and we hurried in that direction, as experience had taught me that the German Forward Observation Officers often did their spotting for the guns from the front-line trench on the flank of the bombarded area.

Sure enough, we soon picked up one of those large dark artillery periscopes, shaped like an armadillo. It was being operated by two men, as far as could be seen. One of them wore a very high peaked cap, and was at once called "Little Willie"; the other had a black beard. The nearest point to which we could approach was more like five than four hundred yards, and though we waited till dark, Little Willie did not show more than his huge cap peak and an inch or two of forehead. As evening fell, we went out of the trenches without having fired, as soon after our arrival the bombardment had ceased, and Little Willie never gave a good target, and the bearded man had disappeared. I did not wish to disturb the German F.O.O.'s in their post; as, now that they were discovered, arrangements could be made to deal with them when next they were observing.

The opportunity occurred three days later, when, after a very long vigil, an officer shot Little Willie, and the same evening a Howitzer battery wiped out the post for good and all.

As, when Little Willie met his end, he was just in the act of spotting the first shots for his battery, which had opened on our front line trenches, his death probably saved us some casualties, for it temporarily stopped the activities of his guns.

It was not only the number of the enemy that our snipers shot that was so important. It was often the psychological moment at which they shot them that gave their work an extra value.

In the autumn of 1915 there came high winds following frosty nights. It was clear that a heavy fall of the leaf would take place on the following days. I therefore asked, and obtained leave from the 4th Division, to which I was at the time attached, to drop instructional work, and instead to go into the trenches in order to spot enemy snipers and artillery observation officers' posts. On my way down I called at Headquarters, where I was told that a very troublesome sniper was operating at Beaumont Hamel. This man had killed a number of our fellows. He was supposed to live in a pollarded willow, one of a row not very far from Jacob's Ladder, which will be remembered by all who were on that front in 1915. There was on that day a certain amount of mild shelling of the communication trenches, but before the advent of gas-shells this rarely caused trouble in the daytime, except to those who had to repair the breaches.

On the day in question I was alone with my batman, who, I can say, without fear of libel, shot better than he batted, for he had been chosen because he was a marksman. Arrived in the front line, we at once set about trying to locate the sniper. As a rule, in such a case, the enemy one seeks is taking a siesta, but this was not so now, for as soon as I looked over the parapet a bullet, striking low, knocked some dust into my eyes. At this point, you must understand, our trenches were shaped like an arm, with a crooked elbow, the crook or turn of the elbow being at the bottom of a hill. In front lay Beaumont Hamel, where in the German lines when

I arrived a soldier had hung out his shirt to dry. Between us and Beaumont Hamel lay a wild piece of No Man's Land, with some dead ground on the Beaumont Hamel side, and at the bottom of the hill the row of willows from which the sniper was supposed to operate.

As these willow trees were out of sight from the place where I had been fired at, I did not put down that shot to the sniper, whom we will call Ernst. In this I was probably wrong, as transpired later.

All that morning we tried to locate Ernst, who had four more shots at me, but all that I had learned at the end of it (when I imagine Ernst went off for a well-earned siesta) was that he was a good shot, as though obviously some distance away, he had made quite good practice. We most carefully examined the pollarded willows, and spotted one or two good snipers' posts, especially one at the bottom of a hedge, but as far as Ernst was concerned he had all the honours.

The next day I was occupied all the morning with an enemy artillery O.P. which was destroyed by howitzer fire, and it was not till after lunch that I could turn my attention once more to Ernst.

This time I began at the bottom of the hill. There were no loopholes, so it was a case of looking over, and almost at once Ernst put in a very close shot, followed again by a second which was not so good. The first shot had cut the top of the parapet just beside my head, and I noticed that several shots had been fired which had also cut the top of the sandbags. Behind the line of these shots was a group of trees, and as they stood on slightly higher ground I crawled to them, and at once saw something of great interest. In the bole of one of the trees a number of bullets had lodged, all within a small circle. Crouching at the base of the tree, and with my head covered with an old sandbag, I raised it until I could see over the parapet fifty yards in front, and found at once that the line of these shots, and those which had struck the tree behind my head, were very nearly the same, and must have been fired from an area of No Man's Land, behind which it looked as if dead ground existed on the enemy's side, and probably from a large bush which formed the most salient feature of that view.

I then went back to the trenches, and warned all sentries to keep a good look-out on this bush and the vicinity. Very soon one of them reported movement in the bush. With my glass I could see a periscope about three feet above the ground in the bush, which was very thick. Being certain, as the periscope was raised so high, and as it had only just been elevated, that it was held in human hands, I collected half a dozen riflemen and my batman, and giving them the range, and the centre of the bush as a target, ordered them to open fire. On the volley the periscope flew backwards and the activities of Ernst ceased forthwith.

It was this experience of looking along the path of the enemy's bullets that led directly to the invention for spotting enemy snipers.

No one can deny that Ernst was a gallant fellow, lying out as he did between the lines day after day. Whether he was killed or not who can say, but I should think the odds are that some bullets of the volley found their billet. At any rate, sniping from that quarter ceased.

I have now given enough description of the work and training which was going on at that time in the Third Army in the line. The aim and end of all this work was the formation of sniping sections in each battalion, consisting of sixteen privates with two N.C.O.s under an officer.

I had realized that my whole problem turned upon the officer. If I could succeed in obtaining fifteen or twenty officers who would be simply fanatics in their work, it was perfectly clear that the sniping movement would spread like wildfire throughout the Army. Already we had got together an immense amount of detail concerning the German sniping organization and had begun not only to challenge his superiority, but also to enforce our own. It is wonderful what can be done in a single week by sixteen accurate shots along the length of line held by a battalion.

You must understand also that the success of the German sniping rested largely upon the deeds of certain crack snipers, who thoroughly understood their work, and who each one of them caused us heavy casualties. The first work to be done in the trenches was the organized annihilation of these skilled German snipers, and I think this was the easier in that they had it their own way for so long.

As time went on, the reports from the brigades were very good; one Brigadier even going so far as to wire me: "Only one Hun sniper left on my front. Can you lend me your elephant rifle?" In this particular brigade the Brigadier informed me that he had not lost a man through enemy sniping in four months.

Sniping, I think, or let us say the sniping campaign, may be divided into four parts. During the first, the Germans had the mastery. During the second, our first aim was to kill off the more dangerous German snipers and to train our own to become more formidable. The third was when the Germans had fairly gone to ground and would no longer give us a chance. The idea now was to invent various ways in which to induce them to give a target, and the final period came at a much later date, when great battles were being fought, and the work of sniping was beginning to merge into that of scouting, and snipers were being trained in great numbers to deal with the new situations that were arising every day as the Germans altered their tactical plans of defence.

CHAPTER EIGHT

The Sharpshooters of Vermont:
A Civil War Account

William Y. W. Ripley

Abate the edge of traitors, gracious Lord.
That would reduce these bloody days again,
And make poor England weep in streams of blood!
Let them not live to taste this land's increase,
That would with treason wound this fair land's peace!
Now civil wounds are stopp'd, peace lives again;
That she may long live here, God say—Amen!
                                                   —KING RICHARD III

VERY SOON AFTER THE OUTBREAK OF THE WAR FOR THE UNION, IMME-
diately, in fact, upon the commencement of actual operations in the
field, it became painfully apparent that, however inferior the rank and
file of the Confederate armies were in point of education and general
intelligence to the men who composed the armies of the Union, however
imperfect and rude their equipment and material, man for man they were
the superiors of their northern antagonists in the use of arms.

Recruited mainly from the rural districts (for the South had but
few large cities from which to draw its fighting strength), their armies
were composed mainly of men who had been trained to the skillful use
of the rifle in that most perfect school, the field and forest, in the pursuit of the game so abundant in those sparsely settled districts. These
men, who came to the field armed at first, to a large extent, with their

favorite sporting or target rifles, and with a training acquired in such a school, were individually more than the equals of the men of the North, who were with comparatively few exceptions, drawn from the farm, the workshop, the office or the counter, and whose life-long occupations had been such as to debar them from those pursuits in which the men of the South had gained their skill. Indeed, there were in many regiments in the northern armies men who had never even fired a gun of any description at the time of their enlistment.

On the other hand, there were known to be scattered throughout the loyal states, a great number of men who had made rifle shooting a study, and who, by practice on the target ground and at the country shooting matches, had gained a skill equal to that of the men of the South in any kind of shooting, and in long range practice a much greater degree of excellency.

There were many of these men in the ranks of the loyal army, but their skill was neutralized by the fact that the arms put into their hands, although the most perfect military weapons then known, were not of the description calculated to show the best results in the hands of expert marksmen.

Occasionally a musket would be found that was accurate in its shooting qualities, and occasionally such a gun would fall into the hands of a man competent to appreciate and utilize its best features. It was speedily found that such a gun, in the hands of such a man, was capable of results not possible to be obtained from a less accurate weapon in the hands of a less skillful man. To remedy this state of affairs, and to make certain that the best weapons procurable should be placed in the hands of the men best fitted to use them effectively, it was decided by the war department, early in the summer of 1861, that a regiment should be organized, to be called the First Regiment of United States Sharp Shooters, and to consist of the best and most expert rifle shots in the Northern States. The detail of the recruiting and organization of this regiment was entrusted to Hiram Berdan, then a resident of the city of New York, himself an enthusiastic lover of rifle shooting, and an expert marksman.

Col. Berdan set himself earnestly at work to recruit and organize such a body of men as should, in the most perfect manner, illustrate the capacity for warlike purposes of his favorite weapon.

It was required that a recruit should possess a good moral character, a sound physical development, and in other respects come within the usual requirements of the army regulations; but, as the men were designed for an especial service, it was required of them that before enlistment they should justify their claim to be called "sharp shooters" by such a public exhibition of their skill as should fairly entitle them to the name, and warrant a reasonable expectation of usefulness in the field. To insure this it was ordered that no recruit be enlisted who could not, in a public trial, make a string of ten shots at a distance of two hundred yards, the aggregate measurement of which should not exceed fifty inches. In other words, it was required that the recruit should, in effect, be able to place ten bullets in succession within a ten-inch ring at a distance of two hundred yards.

Any style of rifle was allowed—telescopic sights, however, being disallowed—and the applicant was allowed to shoot from any position he chose, only being required to shoot from the shoulder.

Circular letters setting forth these conditions, and Col. Berdan's authority, were issued to the governors of the loyal states, and, as a first result from the state of Vermont, Capt. Edmund Weston of Randolph applied for and received of Gov. Holbrook authority to recruit one company of sharp shooters, which was mustered into the service as Co. F, First United States Sharp Shooters, and is the subject of this history.

Capt. Weston at once put himself in communication with well-known riflemen in different parts of the state and appointed recruiting officers in various towns to receive applications and superintend the trials of skill, without which no person could be accepted.

The response was more hearty and more general than could have been expected, and many more recruits presented themselves than could be accepted—many of whom, however, failed to pass the ordeal of the public competition—and, as the event proved, more were accepted than could be legally mustered into the service.

All who were accepted, however, fully met the rigid requirements as to skill in the use of the rifle.

The company rendezvoused at Randolph early in September, 1861, and on the 13th of that month were mustered into the state service by

Charles Dana. The organization of the company as perfected at this time was as follows:

Captain,	Edmund Weston.
First Lieutenant,	C. W. Seaton.
Second Lieutenant,	M. V. B. Bronson.
First Sergeant,	H. E. Kinsman.
Second Sergeant,	E. W. Hindes.
Third Sergeant,	Amos H. Bunker.
Fourth Sergeant,	Milo C. Priest.
Fifth Sergeant,	L. J. Allen.
First Corporal,	Daniel Perry.
Second Corporal,	Fred. E. Streeter.
Third Corporal,	Ai Brown.
Fourth Corporal,	W. C. Kent.
Fifth Corporal,	H. J. Peck.
Sixth Corporal,	W. H. Tafft.
Seventh Corporal,	C. D. Merriman.
Eighth Corporal,	C. W. Peck.
Bugler,	Calvin Morse.
Wagoner,	Edward F. Stevens.

Thus organized, the company, with one hundred and thirteen enlisted men, left the state on the same day on which they were mustered, and proceeded via New Haven and Long Island Sound to the rendezvous of the regiment at Weehawken Heights, near New York, where they went into camp with other companies of the regiment which had preceded them. On or about the 24th of September the regiment proceeded under orders from the war department to Washington, arriving at that city at a late hour on the night of the twenty-fifth, and were assigned quarters at the Soldiers' Rest, so well known to the troops who arrived at Washington at about that time. On the twenty-sixth they were ordered to a permanent camp of instruction well out in the country and near the residence and grounds of Mr. Corcoran, a wealthy resident of Washington of supposed secession proclivities, where they were for the first time in a regularly organized camp, and could begin to feel that they were fairly cut off at last from the customs and habits of civil life. Here they were regularly mustered into the service of the United States, thirteen enlisted men being rejected, however, to reduce the company to the regulation complement of one hundred enlisted men; so that of the one hundred and thirteen men charged to the company on the rolls of the Adjutant and Inspector General of Vermont, only one hundred took the field. Other companies from different states arrived at about the same time, and the regiment was at last complete, having its full complement of ten companies of one hundred men each.

The field and staff at this time was made up as follows:

Colonel,	H. Berdan.
Lieutenant-Colonel,	Frederick Mears.
Major,	W. S. Rowland.
Adjutant,	Floyd A. Willett.
Quarter-Master,	W. H. Beebe.
Surgeon,	G. C. Marshall.
Assistant Surgeon,	Dr. Brennan.
Chaplain,	Rev. Dr. Coit.

Only one of the field officers had had a military education or military experience. Lieutenant-Colonel Mears was an officer of the regular army, a thorough drill master and a strict disciplinarian. Under his efficient command the regiment soon began to show a marked and daily improvement that augured well for its future usefulness. The officers of the regimental staff were, each in his own department, able and painstaking men. The chaplain alone was not quite popular among the rank and file, and they rather envied the Second Regiment of Sharp Shooters who were encamped near them, and whose chaplain, the Rev. Lorenzo Barber, was the beau ideal of an army chaplain. Tender hearted and kind, he was ever ready to help the weak and the suffering; now dressing a wound and now helping along a poor fellow, whose fingers were all thumbs and whose thoughts were too big for utterance (on paper), with his letter to the old mother at home; playing ball or running a foot race, beating the best marksmen at the targets, and finally preaching a rousing good sermon which was attentively listened to on Sunday. His *faith* was in the "Sword of the Lord and of Gideon," but his best *work* was put in with a twenty pound telescopic rifle which he used with wonderful effect. The original plan of armament contemplated the use exclusively of target or sporting rifles. The men had been encouraged to bring with them their favorite weapons, and had been told that the government would pay for such arms at the rate of sixty dollars each, while those who chose to rely upon the United States armories for their rifles were to be furnished with the best implements procurable. The guns to be so furnished were to be breach loaders, to have telescopic sights, hair triggers, and all the requisites for the most perfect shooting that the most skillful marksman could desire.

Many of the men had, with this understanding, brought with them their own rifles, and with them target shooting became a pastime, and many matches between individuals and companies were made and many very short strings were recorded.

Under the stimulus of competition and organized practice great improvement was noted in marksmanship, even among those who had been considered almost perfect marksmen before. On one occasion President Lincoln, accompanied by Gen. McClellan, paid a visit to the camp and asked to be allowed to witness some of the sharp shooting of which he had heard so much.

A detail of the best men was made and a display of skill took place which, perhaps, was never before equalled. President Lincoln himself, as did Gen. McClellan, Col. Hudson and others of the staff, took part in the firing, the President using a rifle belonging to Corporal H. J. Peck of the Vermont company.

At the close of the exhibition Col. Berdan, being asked to illustrate the accuracy of his favorite rifle, fired three shots at different portions of the six hundred yard target; when having satisfied himself that he had the proper range, and that both himself and rifle could be depended upon, announced that at the next shot he would strike the right eye of the gaily colored Zouave which, painted on the half of an A tent, did duty for a target at that range. Taking a long and careful aim, he fired, hitting the exact spot selected and announced beforehand. Whether partly accidental or not it was certainly a wonderful performance and placed Col. Berdan at once in the foremost rank of rifle experts. On the 28th of November, the day set apart by the governors of the loyal states as Thanksgiving Day, shooting was indulged by in different men of Co. F and other companies for a small prize offered by the field officers, the terms being two hundred yards, off hand, the shortest string of two shots to win. The prize was won from a large number of skillful contestants by Ai Brown of Co. F—his two shots measuring 4⅛ inches, or each within 2⅛ inches of the center.

On the 7th of December another regimental shooting match took place; the prize going this time to a Michigan man, his string of three shots, fired off hand at two hundred yards, measuring six inches. These records are introduced here simply for the purpose of showing the wonderful degree of skill possessed by these picked marksmen in the use of the rifle. But it was soon found that there were objections to the use in the field of the fine guns so effective on the target ground. The great weight of some of them was of itself almost prohibitory, for, to a soldier burdened with the weight of his knapsack, haversack and canteen, blanket and overcoat, the additional weight of a target rifle—many of which weighed fifteen pounds each, and some as much as thirty pounds—was too much to be easily borne.

It was also found difficult to provide the proper ammunition for such guns in the field, and finally, owing to the delicacy of the construction of the sights, hair triggers, etc., they were constantly liable to be out of order, and when thus disabled, of even less use than the smooth-bore musket, with buck and ball cartridge of fifty years before. Manufacturers of fine guns from all parts of our own country, and many from Europe, flocked to the camp of the sharp shooters offering their goods, each desirous of the credit of furnishing arms to a body of men so well calculated to use them effectively, and many fine models were offered. The choice of the men, however, seemed to be a modified military rifle made by the Sharpe Rifle Manufacturing Co., and a request was made to the war department for a supply of these arms. At this early day, however, the departments were full of men whose ideas and methods were those of a half a century gone by; and at the head of the ordnance department was a man who, in addition to being of this stamp, was the father of the muzzle loading Springfield rifle, then the recognized arm of the United States Infantry, and from him came the most strenuous opposition to the proposal to depart from the traditions of the regular army.

Gen. McClellan, and even the President himself, were approached on this subject, and both recognized the propriety of the proposed style of armament and the great capacity for efficient service possessed by the regiment when it should be once satisfactorily armed and fairly in front of the enemy. But the ordnance department was ever a block in the way; its head obstinately and stubbornly refusing to entertain any proposition other than to arm the regiment with the ordinary army musket; and, to add to the growing dissatisfaction among the men over the subject of arms, it became known that the promises made to them at the time of enlistment, that the government would pay them for their rifles at the rate of sixty dollars each, was unauthorized and would not be fulfilled; and also that the representations made to them with respect to telescopic breech loaders were likewise unauthorized. Discontent became general and demoralization began to show itself in an alarming form.

Some of the field officers were notoriously incompetent; the Major, one of those military adventurers who floated to the surface during the early years of the war, particularly so; he was a kind of a modern Dalgetty without the courage or skill of his renowned prototype, rarely present in camp, and when there of little or no service.

The Lieutenant-Colonel, a man of rare energy and skill in his profession, and whose painstaking care had made the regiment all that it was at that time, fearing the after effects of this demoralization on the efficiency of the command, and seeing opportunity for his talents in other fields, resigned; and on the 29th of November, 1861, Wm. Y. W. Ripley of Rutland, Vt., was appointed Lieutenant-Colonel, and Caspar Trepp, Captain of Co. A., was made Major. Lieutenant-Colonel Ripley had seen service only as Captain of Co. K, First Vermont Volunteers. Major Trepp had received a thorough military training in the army of his native Switzerland, and had seen active service in European wars. The regiment remained at camp of instruction under the immediate command of

Lieut.-Col. Ripley, employed in the usual routine of camp duty, drills, etc., during the whole of the winter of 1861–62, particular attention being paid to the skirmish drill, in which the men became wonderfully proficient; and it is safe to say that for general excellence in drill, except the manual of arms, they were excelled by few volunteer regiments in the service.

All orders were given by the sound of the bugle, and the whole regiment deployed as skirmishers could be as easily maneuvered as a single company could be in line of battle. The bugle corps was under the charge of Calvin Morse of Co. F as chief bugler, and under his careful instruction attained to an unusual degree of excellence. All camp and other calls were sounded on the bugle, and the men found them pleasant little devices for translating curt and often rough English into music. They were bugled to breakfast and to dinner, bugled to guard mounting and bugled to battle, brigades moved and cavalry charged to the sound of the bugle. The men often found fanciful resemblances in the notes of the music to the words intended to be conveyed. Thus, the recall was sung as follows:

"Come back again, come back again,
Come back, come back, come back again."

While the sick call was thus rendered into words:

"Come to qui-nine, come to qui-nine,
Come to qui-i-nine, come to qui-i-nine."

They were not, on the whole, bad translations.

The winter was an unusually severe one, and, as the enemy maintained a strict blockade of the Potomac, the supply of wood was often short, and some suffering was the result. The health of the regiment remained fairly good; measles, small pox, and other forms of camp diseases appeared, however, and Co. F, of course, suffered its share, losing by death from disease during the winter, Wm. T. Battles, Edward Fitz, Sumner E. Gardner and Geo. H. Johnson.

On the 20th of March, 1862, the regiment received orders to report to Major-Gen. Fitz John Porter, whose division then lay at Alexandria,

Va., awaiting transportation to Fortress Monroe to join the army under McClellan. At this time the regiment was without arms of any kind, except for the few target rifles remaining in the hands of their owners, and a few old smooth bore muskets which had been used during the winter for guard duty. Shortly before this time the war department, perhaps wearied by constant importunity, perhaps recognizing the importance of the subject, had so far receded from its former position as to offer to arm the regiment with revolving rifles of the Colt pattern, and had sent the guns to the camp for issue to the men with promise of exchanging them for Sharpe's rifles at a later day.

They were five chambered breech loaders, very pretty to look at, but upon examination and test they were found inaccurate and unreliable, prone to get out of order and even dangerous to the user. They were not satisfactory to the men, who knew what they wanted and were fully confident of their ability to use such guns as they had been led by repeated promises to expect, to good advantage. When, however, news came that the rebels had evacuated Manassas, and that the campaign was about to open in good earnest, they took up these toys, for after all they were hardly more, and turned their faces southward. Co. F was the first company in the regiment to receive their arms, and to the influence of their patriotic example the regiment owes its escape from what at one time appeared to be a most unfortunate embarrassment.

The march to Alexandria over Long Bridge was made in the midst of a pouring rain and through such a sea of mud as only Virginia can afford material for. It was the first time the regiment had ever broken camp, and its first hard march. It was long after dark when the command arrived near Cloud's mills; the headquarters of Gen. Porter could not be found, and it became necessary for the regiment to camp somewhere for the night. At a distance were seen the lights of a camp, which was found upon examination to be the winter quarters of the 69th New York in charge of a camp guard, the regiment having gone out in pursuit of the enemy beyond Manassas. A few persuasive words were spoken to the sergeant in command, and the tired and soaked sharp shooters turned into the tents of the absent Irishmen.

On the 28th of April the Third Corps, to which the sharp shooters were now attached, moved down the river to a point some five miles below Falmouth to support Sedgwick's command which was ordered to cross the Rappahannock at or near the point at which Gen. Franklin had crossed his Grand Division at the battle of Fredericksburgh.

Some days prior to this all surplus clothing and baggage had been turned in. Eight days rations and sixty rounds of ammunition were now issued, and the "finest army on the planet" was foot loose once more. Sedgwick's crossing was made, however, without serious opposition, and on the thirtieth the Third Corps, making a wide detour to the rear to avoid the notice of the watchful enemy, turned northward and on the next day crossed the river at United States ford and took its place in the lines of Chancellorsville with the rest of the army. This great battle has been so often described and in such minute detail that it is not necessary for us to attempt a detailed description of the movements of the different corps engaged, or indeed proper, since this purports to be a history of the marches and battles of only one small company out of the thousands there engaged. It will be remembered that the regiment was now attached to the Third Corps, commanded by Gen. Sickles, the First Division under Gen. Whipple and the Third Brigade, Gen. De Trobriand. At eleven o'clock A.M. on this day, being the first of May, the battle proper commenced, although severe and continuous skirmishing had been going on ever since the first troops crossed the river on the 29th of April. The Third Corps was held in reserve in rear of the Chancellorsville house, having arrived at that point at about the time that the assaulting columns moved forward to the attack. Almost instantly the fighting became furious and deadly. The country was covered with dense undergrowth of stunted cedars, among and over which grew heavy masses of the trailing vines which grow so luxuriantly in that portion of Virginia, and which renders the orderly passage of troops well-nigh impossible. To add to the difficulties which beset the attacking forces, it was impossible to see what was in front of them; hence the first notice of the presence of a rebel line of battle was a volley delivered at short range directly in the faces of the Union soldiers, whose presence and movements were unavoidably made plain to the concealed enemy by the noise made in forcing a passage through the tangled forest.

Notwithstanding these disadvantages the Fifth Corps, with which the sharp shooters had so recently parted, struck the enemy at about a mile distant from the position now held by the Third Corps, and drove them steadily back for a long distance until, having passed far to the front of the general line, Meade found his flank suddenly attacked and was forced to retire. Other columns also met the enemy at about the same distance to the front and met with a like experience, gaining, however, on the whole, substantial ground during the afternoon; and so night closed down on the first day of the battle.

On the morning of the 2d of May a division of the Third Corps was detached to hold a gap in the lines between the Eleventh and Twelfth Corps which Gen. Hooker thought too weak. The sharp shooters, however, remained with the main column near the Chancellorsville house. Early on this day the Confederate Gen. Jackson commenced that wonderful flank march which resulted in the disaster to the Eleventh Corps on the right, later in the day. This march, carefully masked as it was, was, nevertheless, observed by Hooker, who at first supposed it the commencement of a retreat on the part of Lee to Gordonsville, and Gen. Sickles was ordered with the two remaining divisions of his corps to demonstrate in that direction and act as circumstances should determine. In this movement Birney's division had the advance, the first division, under Whipple, being in support of Birney's left flank. The sharp shooters were, however, ordered to report to Gen. Birney, and were by him placed in the front line as skirmishers, although their deployment was at such short intervals that it was more like a single rank line of battle than a line of skirmishers. Sickles started on his advance at about one o'clock P.M., his formation being as above described. Rapidly pressing forward, the sharp shooters passed out of the dense thickets into a comparatively open country, where they could at least breathe more freely and see a little of what was before them. They soon struck a line of rebels in position on the crest of a slight elevation, and brisk firing commenced; the advance, however, not being checked, they soon cleared the hill of the enemy and occupied it themselves. Changing front to the left, the regiment moved from this position obliquely to the southeast, and soon found themselves opposed to a line which had evidently come to stay. The fighting here was very severe and lasted for a considerable time. The rebels seemed to have a desire to stay the advance of the Union troops at that particular point, and for some particular reason, which was afterwards made apparent.

After some minutes of brisk firing, the sharp shooters, by a sudden rush on their flank, succeeded in compelling the surrender of the entire force, which was found to consist of the Twenty-third Georgia regiment, consisting of three hundred and sixty officers and men, which had been charged by Jackson with the duty of preventing any advance of the Union troops at this point which might discover his march towards Hooker's right, hence the tenacity with which they clung to the position.

In this affair Co. F lost Edward Trask and A. D. Griffin, wounded.

The obstruction having been thus removed, the Third Corps, led by the sharp shooters, pressed rapidly forward to the southward as far as Hazel Grove, or the old furnace, some two miles from the place of starting, and far beyond any supporting column which could be depended on for early assistance should such be needed. It had now become apparent to all that Jackson, instead of being in full retreat as had been supposed, was in the full tide of one of the most violent offensives on record; and at five o'clock P.M. Sickles was ordered to attack his right flank and thus check his advance on the exposed right of the army. But at about the same time Sickles found that he was himself substantially cut off from the army, and that it would require the most strenuous efforts to prevent the capture or destruction of his own command. Furthermore, before he could make his dispositions and march over the ground necessary to be traversed before he could reach Jackson's right, that officer had struck his objective point, and the rout of the Eleventh Corps was complete. The most that Sickles could now do, under the circumstances, was to fight his own way back to his supports, and to choose, if possible, such a route as would place him, on his arrival, in a position to check Jackson's further advance and afford the broken right wing an opportunity to rally and regain their organization, which was hopelessly, as it appeared, lost. In the darkness and gloom of the falling night, with unloaded muskets (for in this desperate attempt the bayonet only was to be depended upon), the two divisions of the Third Corps set their faces northwardly, and pressed their way through the tangled undergrowth to the rescue of the endangered right wing.

As usual, the sharp shooters had the advance, and received the first volley from the concealed enemy. They had received no especial orders concerning the use, solely, of the bayonet, and were at once engaged in a close conflict under circumstances in which their only superiority over troops of the line consisted in the advantage of the rapidity of fire afforded by their breech loaders over the muzzle loading rifles opposed to them. Closely supported by the line of Birney's division, and firing as they advanced at the flashes of the opposing guns (for they could see no more), they pushed on until they were fairly intermingled with the rebels, and in many individual instances, a long distance inside the enemy's line, every man fighting for himself—for in this confused melee, in the dense jungle and in the intense darkness of the night, no supervision could be exercised by officers and many shots were fired at distances no greater than a few feet. So they struggled on until, with a hurrah and a grand rush, Birney's gallant men dashed forward with the bayonet alone, and after ten minutes of hand to hand fighting, they succeeded in retaking the plank road, and a considerable portion of the line held by the left of the Eleventh Corps in the early portion of the day and lost in the tremendous charge of Jackson's corps in the early evening. Sickles had cut his way out, and more, he was now in a position to afford the much needed aid to those who so sorely required it. Both parties had fought to the point of exhaustion, and were glad to suspend operations for a time for this cause alone, even had no better reasons offered.

But the Union army was no longer in a position for offense; the extreme left, with which we have had nothing to do, had been so heavily pressed during the afternoon that it had been with difficulty that a disaster similar to the one which had overtaken the right had been prevented on that flank, and in the center, at and about Hazel Grove and the furnace, which had been held by Sickles, and from which he had been ordered to the support of the right as we have seen, an absolute gap existed, covered by no force whatever. This, then, was the situation, briefly stated.

The left was barely able to hold its own, the center was absolutely abandoned, and the right had been utterly routed. In this state of affairs the Union commander was in no mood for a further offense at that time. On the other hand, the controlling mind that had conceived, and thus far had successfully carried out this wonderful attack which had been so disastrous to the Union army, and which bade fair to make the Southern Confederacy a fact among the nations, had been stricken down in the full tide of its success. Stonewall Jackson had been wounded at about nine o'clock by the fire of his own men. He had passed beyond the lines of his pickets to reconnoiter the Union position, and on his return with his staff they were mistaken by his soldiers for a body of federal cavalry and he received three wounds from the effects of which he died about a week later. So fell a man who was perhaps as fine a type of stout American soldiership as any produced on either side during the war.

The sharp shooters, with the remnant of the Third Corps, passed the remainder of the night on the plank road near Dowdall's tavern. Co. F had left their knapsacks and blankets under guard near the Chancellorsville house when they advanced from that point in the morning, as had the rest of the regiment. Under these circumstances little sleep or rest could be expected even had the enemy been in less close proximity. But with the rebel pickets hardly thirty yards distant, and firing at every thing they saw or heard, sleep was out of the question. So passed the weary night of the disastrous 2d of May at Chancellorsville.

During the night Gen. Hooker, no longer on the offensive, had been busily engaged in laying out and fortifying a new line on which he might hope more successfully to resist the attack which all knew must come at an early hour on the morning of the third. On the extreme left the troops were withdrawn from their advanced positions to a more compact and shorter line in front of, and to the south and east of the Chancellorsville house. The center, which at sunset was unoccupied by any considerable body of Union troops, was made secure; and at daylight Sickles, with the Third Corps, was ordered to withdraw to a position indicated immediately in front of Fairview, a commanding height of land now strongly occupied by the Union artillery. It was not possible, however, to withdraw so large a body of troops from their advanced position, in the face of so watchful an enemy, without interruption. In fact, even before the movement had commenced, the enemy took the initiative and commenced the battle of that day by a furious attack upon the heights of Hazel Grove, the position so handsomely won by the Third Corps on the previous day and from which they were ordered to the relief of the Eleventh Corps at five o'clock on the preceding afternoon, as we have seen. This height of land commanded almost every portion of the field occupied by the Union army, and from it Sickles' line, as it stood at daybreak, could be completely enfiladed. This position was held by an inadequate force for its defense; indeed, as it was far in advance of the new line of battle it may be supposed that observation, rather than defense, was the duty of its occupants. They made a gallant fight, however, but were soon compelled to retire with the loss of four guns. The rebel commander, quick to see the great importance of the position, crowned the hill with thirty guns which, with the four taken from the Unionists, poured a heavy fire on all parts of the line, devoting particular attention to Sickles' exposed left and rear.

At almost the same period of time the rebels in Sickles' front made a savage attack on his line. The men of the Third Corps fought, as they always fought, stubbornly and well, but, with a force more than equal to their own in point of numbers, flushed with their success of the previous afternoon and burning to avenge the fall of Jackson, in their front, and this enormous concentration of artillery hammering away on their defenseless left, they were at last forced back to the new line in front of Fairview.

In preparation for the withdrawal contemplated, and before the rebel attack developed itself, the sharp shooters had been deployed to the front and formed a skirmish line to the north of the plank road with their left on that highway, and thus received the first of the rebel attack. They succeeded in repulsing the advance of the first line and for half an hour held their ground against repeated attempts of the rebel skirmishers to dislodge them. The position they held was one of the utmost importance since it commanded the plank road which must be the main line of the rebel approach to Fairview, the key to the new Union line, and aware of this the men fought on with a courage and determination seldom witnessed even in the ranks of that gallant regiment. After half an hour of this perilous work, the regiment on their right having given way, the sharp shooters were ordered to move by the right flank to cover the interval thus exposed, their own place being taken by still another body of infantry. Steadily and coolly the men faced to the right at the sound of the bugle, and commenced their march, still firing as they advanced. Necessarily, however, the men had to expose themselves greatly in this movement, and as necessarily their own fire was less effective than when delivered coolly from the shelter of some friendly tree, log or bank which skirmishers are so prone to seek and so loath to leave. Still the march was made in good order and in good time, for the sharp shooters had only just time to fill the gap when the rebels came on for a final trial for the mastery.

For a long time the green coated riflemen clung to their ground and gave, certainly as good, as they received. But the end of the long struggle was at hand; the regiment which had taken the position just vacated by the sharp shooters was driven in confusion, and to cap the climax of misfortune, the Union artillery, observing the withdrawal of other troops, and supposing that all had been retired, opened a furious fire of canister into the woods.

The sharp shooters were now in a sad case—before them a furious crowd of angry enemies, on the left the rebel artillery at Hazel Grove sweeping their lines from left to right at every discharge, while, worst of all, from the rear came the equally dangerous fire of their own friends. To retreat was as bad as to advance. The ground to their right was an unknown mystery and no hopeful sign came from the left; so taking counsel from their very desperation they concluded to remain just there, at least until some reasonable prospect of escape should present itself. Taking such cover as they could get, some from the fire of our own guns and some from those of the rebels, shifting from side to side of the logs and trees as the fire came hotter from the one side or from the other, but always keeping up their own fire in the direction of the enemy, they maintained the unequal fight until an officer, sent for the purpose, succeeded in stopping the fire of our own guns, and the sharp shooters willingly withdrew from a position such as they had never found themselves in before, and from a scene which no man present will ever forget.

They were sharply pressed by the advancing enemy, but now, being out of the line of the enfilading fire from Hazel Grove, and no longer subject to the fire of their own friends, the withdrawal was made in perfect order, the line halting at intervals at the sound of the bugle and delivering well aimed volleys at the enemy, now fully exposed, and even at times making countercharges to check their too rapid advance.

In one of these rallies there fell a man from another company whose death as well deserves to be remembered in song as that of the "Sleeping Sentinel." He had been condemned to death by the sentence of a court martial, and was in confinement awaiting the execution of the sentence when the army left camp at Falmouth at the outset of the campaign. In some manner he managed to escape from his guards, and joined his company on the evening of the second day's light. Of course it was irregular, and no precedent for it could possibly be found in the army regulations, but men were more valuable on that field than in the guard house; perhaps, too, his captain hoped that he might, in the furor of the battle, realize his own expressed wish that he might meet his fate there instead of at the hands of a firing party of the provost guard, and thus, by an honorable death on the battle field, efface to some extent the stain on his character. However it was, a rifle was soon found for him (rifles without owners were plenty on that field), and he took his place in the ranks.

During all of that long forenoon's fighting he was a marked man. All knew his history, and all watched to see him fall; for while others carefully availed themselves of such shelter as the field afforded, he alone stood erect and in full view of the enemy. Many times he exhausted the cartridges in his box, each time replenishing it from the boxes of his dead or wounded companions. He seemed to bear a charmed life; for, while death and wounds came to many who would have avoided either, the bullets passed him harmless by. At last, however, in one of the savage conflicts when the sharp shooters turned on the too closely following enemy, this gallant soldier, with two or three of his companions, came suddenly upon a small party of rebels who had outstripped their fellows in the ardor of the pursuit; he, being in the advance, rushed upon them, demanding their surrender. "Yes," said one, "we surrender," but at the same time, as —— lowered his gun, the treacherous rebel raised his, and the sharp shooter fell, shot through the heart. He spoke no word, but those who caught the last glimpse of his face, as they left him lying where he fell, knew that he had realized his highest hope and wish, and that he died content.

The sequel to this sad personal history brings into tender recollection the memory of that last and noblest martyr to the cause of the Union, President Lincoln. The case was brought to his notice by those who felt that the stain upon the memory of this gallant, true hearted soldier was not fully effaced, even by his noble self-sacrifice, and would not be while the records on the books stood so black against him. The President was never appealed to in vain when it was possible for him to be merciful, and, sitting down, he wrote with his own hand a full and free pardon, dating it as of the morning of that eventful 3d of May, and sent it to the widow of the dead soldier in a distant state. It was such acts as this that made Abraham Lincoln so loved by the soldiers of the Union. They respected the President, but Abraham Lincoln—the man—was *loved*.

Upon the arrival of the retreating riflemen at the new line in front of Fairview, they found their division, the main portion of which had, of course, preceded them, in line of battle in rear of the slight defenses which had been thrown up at that point, where they enjoyed a brief period of much needed repose, if a short respite from actual personal encounter could be called repose. They were still under heavy artillery fire, while musketry was incessant and very heavy only a short distance away, the air above their heads being alive, at times, with everything that kills. Yet so great was their fatigue, and so quiet and restful their position in comparison with what it had been for so long a time, that, after receiving rations and a fresh supply of ammunition for their exhausted boxes, officers and men alike lay down on the ground, and most of them enjoyed an hour of refreshing sleep.

"Use doth breed a habit in a man."

Their rest was not of long duration, however, for the rebels made a desperate and savage attack on the line in their front and the Third Corps soon found itself again engaged. The enemy, under cover of their artillery on the high ground at Hazel Grove, made an assault on what was now the front of the Union line (if it could be said to have a front), while the force which the sharp shooters had so long held in check during the early part of the day made a like attack on that line now the right of the entire army. So heavy was the attack, and so tenaciously sustained, that the Union troops were actually forced from their lines in front and on the flank of Fairview, and the hill was occupied by the rebels, who captured, and held for a time, all the Union guns on that eminence. It was at this stage of affairs that the Third Corps was again called into action, and charging the somewhat disorganized enemy they retook the hill with the captured guns, and following up the flying rebels, they drove them to, and beyond the position they had occupied in the morning.

Here, however, meeting with a fresh line of the enemy and being brought to a check, they were ordered again to retire; for Hooker, by this time intent only upon getting his army safely back across the river, had formed still another new line near to, and covering, the bridges and fords by which alone could he place his forces in a position of even comparative safety. To this line then the Third Corps, with the tired and decimated sharp shooters, retired late in the afternoon, hoping and praying for a respite from their terrible labors. For a little time it looked, indeed, as if their hopes would be realized, but as darkness drew on the corps commander, desiring to occupy a wooded knoll at some little distance from his advanced picket line, and from which he anticipated danger, ordered Gen. Whipple, to whose division the sharp shooters had been returned, to send a brigade to occupy it. Gen. Whipple replied that he had one regiment who were alone equal to the task and to whom he would entrust it, and ordered the sharp shooters to attempt it.

Between this wooded hill and the position from which the regiment must charge was an open field about one hundred yards in width which was to be crossed under what might prove a destructive fire from troops already occupying the coveted position. It was a task requiring the most undaunted courage and desperate endeavor on the part of men who had already been for two full days and nights in the very face of the enemy, and they felt that the attempt might fairly have been assigned to a portion of the forty thousand men who, up to that time, had been held in reserve by Gen. Hooker for some inscrutable purpose, and who had not seen the face of an enemy, much less fired a shot at them; but they formed for the assault with cheerful alacrity. To Co. F was assigned the lead, and marching out into the open field they deployed as regularly as though on their old drill ground at camp of instruction. Corps, brigade and division commanders were looking on, and the men felt that now, if never before, they must show themselves worthy sons of the Green Mountain state.

Led by their officers, they dashed out into the plain closely supported by the rest of the regiment. Night was rapidly coming on, and in the gathering gloom objects could hardly be distinguished at a distance of a hundred yards. Half the open space was crossed, and it seemed to the rushing men that their task was to be accomplished without serious obstructions, when, from the edge of the woods in front, came a close and severe volley betraying the presence of a rebel line of battle; how strong could only be judged by the firing, which was so heavy, however, as to indicate a force much larger than the attacking party. On went the brave men of Co. F, straight at their work, and behind them closely followed the supporting force. In this order they reached the edge of the forest when the enemy, undoubtedly supposing from the confidence with which the sharp shooters advanced that the force was much larger than it really was, broke and fled and the position was won.

From prisoners and wounded rebels captured in that night attack it was learned that the force which had thus been beaten out of a strong position by this handful of men was a portion of the famous Stonewall brigade, Jackson's earliest command, and they asserted that it was the first time in the history of the brigade that it had ever been driven from a chosen position. The sharp shooters were justly elated at their success and the more so when Gen. Whipple, riding over to the point so gallantly won, gave them unstinted praise for their gallant action. In this affair the regiment lost many gallant officers and men, among whom were Lieut. Brewer of Co. C and Capt. Chase, killed, and Major Hastings and Adjt. Horton, wounded. In Co. F Michael Cunningham, J. S. Bailey and E. M. Hosmer were wounded.

Major Hastings had not been a popular officer with the command. Although a brave and capable man, he was of a nervous temperament, and in the small details of camp discipline was apt to be over zealous at times. He had, therefore, incurred the dislike of many men, who were wont to apply various opprobrious epithets to him at such times and under such circumstances as made it extremely unpleasant for him. Such were the methods adopted by some soldiers to make it uncomfortable for officers to whom they had a dislike.

In the case of the Major, however, this was a thing of the past. On this bloody field the men learned to respect their officer, and he, as he was borne from the field, freely forgave the boys all the trouble and annoyance they had caused him, in consideration of their gallant bearing on that day. Adjt. Horton, also a brave and efficient officer, received a severe wound—which afterwards cost him his good right arm—while using the rifle of J. S. Bailey of Co. F, who had been wounded.

Co. F, which, it will be remembered, had been acting as skirmishers, were pushed forward in advance of the main portion of the regiment to further observe the movements of the enemy and to guard against a surprise, and shortly afterwards were moved by the flank some two hundred yards to the right, and were soon after relieved by a force of infantry of the line which had been sent up for that purpose. While retiring toward the position to which they were directed, they passed nearly over the same ground which they had just vacated when they moved by the right flank, as previously mentioned, and received from the concealed rebels, who had reoccupied the line, a severe volley at close range. Facing to the right, Co. F at once charged this new enemy and drove them in confusion from the field. Lying down in this advanced position they passed the remainder of the night in watchful suspense.

At day break on the fourth day of the battle, Co. F was relieved from its position on the picket line and returned to the regiment, which was deployed as skirmishers, and led the van of Whipple's division in a charge to check movements of the enemy which had for their apparent object the interposition of a rebel force between the right wing of the army and its bridges. Firing rapidly as they advanced, and supported by the division close on their heels, they drove the enemy from their rifle pits, which were occupied by the infantry of the Third Corps, the sharp shooters being still in front. Here they remained, exchanging occasional shots with the rebel sharp shooters as occasion offered, for some hours. Hooker was not minded to force the fighting at Chancellorsville; preferring to await the result of Sedgwick's battle at Salem Church, which had raged furiously on the preceding afternoon until darkness put an end to the strife, and the tell tale guns of which even now gave notice of further effort.

Lee, however, pugnacious and aggressive, determined to renew his attack on the right, and, if possible, secure the roads to the fords and bridges by which alone could the defeated army regain the north bank of the river. With this view he reenforced Jackson's (now Stuart's) corps, and organized a powerful attack on the position of the Third Corps. The force of the first onset fell on the sharp shooters, who fought with their accustomed gallantry, but were forced by the weight of numbers back to the main line. Here the fighting was severe and continuous. The one party fighting for a decisive victory, and the other, alas, only bent on keeping secure its last and only line of retreat; but the incentive, poor as it was, was sufficient, and the rebels were unable to break the line. After four hours of continued effort they abandoned the assault and quiet once more prevailed. In this fight Gen. Whipple, the division commander, was killed. He was a gallant and an able soldier, greatly beloved by his men for the kindliness of his disposition. He had an especial liking for and confidence in the sharp shooters, which was fully understood and appreciated by them, and they felt his death as a personal loss.

To add to the horrors of this bloody field, on which lay nearly nine thousand dead and wounded Union soldiers and nearly or quite as many rebels, the woods took fire and hundreds of badly wounded men, unable to help themselves, and hopeless of succor, perished miserably in the fierce flames. Nothing in the whole history of the war is more horrible than the recollection of those gallant men, who had been stricken down by rebel bullets, roasted to death in the very presence of their comrades, impotent to give them aid in their dire distress and agony.

"Oh, happy *dead* who early fell."

It was reserved for the *wounded* to experience the agonies of a tenfold death. Hour after hour the conflagration raged, until a merciful rain quenched it and put an end to the horrible scene. The Third Corps remained in their position during the night, the sharp shooters, oddly enough as it seemed to them, with a strong line of infantry behind works between them and the enemy. Nothing occurred to break their repose, and for the first time for seven days they enjoyed eight hours of solid sleep unbroken by rebel alarms.

At day break on the morning of the 5th of May they were aroused by the usual command of "sharp shooters to the front," and again found themselves on the picket line confronting the enemy. The day passed, however, without serious fighting, one or two attacks being made by rebel skirmishers, more, apparently, to ascertain if the Union troops were actually there than for any more serious business.

These advances were easily repulsed by the sharp shooters without other aid, and at nine o'clock P.M., after seventeen hours of continuous duty without rations—for the eight days rations with which they started from their camp at Falmouth had long since been exhausted, and the scanty supply they had received on the afternoon of the third was barely enough for one meal—they were relieved and retired to the main line. The company lost on this day but one man, Martin C. Laffie, shot through the hand. Laffie was permanently disabled by his wound, and on the 1st of the following August was transferred to the Invalid Corps and never rejoined the company. Several prisoners were captured by the men of Co. F on that day, but on the whole it was, as compared with the days of the preceding week, uneventful. On the 6th the army recrossed the Rappahannock by the bridges which had been preserved by the stubborn courage of the Third Corps, and the battle of Chancellorsville passed into history. The sharp shooters returned to their old camp at Falmouth as they had returned to the same camp after the disastrous battle of Fredericksburgh. It seemed as though they were fated never to leave that ground to fight a successful battle. Only eight days before they had marched out with buoyant anticipations, full of courage and full of hope. They returned discouraged and dispirited beyond description.

At Fredericksburgh the army had marched to the attack without hope or expectation of victory, for their soldiers' instinct told them that that was impossible. At Chancellorsville, however, they felt that they had everything to hope for—a magnificent army in full health and high spirits, an able and gallant commander, for such he had always shown himself to be, and a fair field. The thickets of the wilderness, it is true, were dense and well nigh impassable for them, but they were as bad for the enemy as for themselves, and they had felt that on anything like a fair field they ought to win. Now they found themselves just where they started; they had left seventeen thousand of their comrades dead, or worse than dead, on the field, and fourteen guns remained in the hands of the rebels as trophies of their victory; guns, too, that were sure to be turned against the federals in the very next battle. Twenty thousand stand of small arms were also left on the field to be gathered up by the victors. It was a disheartening reflection, but soldier-like the men put it from their thoughts and turned their minds and hands to the duties and occupations of the present.

In this battle Co. F lost Edward Trask, Jacob S. Bailey, Almon D. Griffin, Martin C. Laffie and John Monahan, wounded, besides several more whose names do not now occur to the writer. Bailey had been previously wounded at Malvern Hill and on this occasion his wound necessitated the amputation of his left arm, and he was honorably discharged from the service on the twenty-sixth of the following August. Monahan was transferred to the Invalid Corps and Griffin returned to his company and remained with it to be honorably mustered out by reason of expiration of term of service, on the 13th of September, 1864. Trask returned to his company to serve with it until the 5th of May, 1864, when he was killed in the battle of the Wilderness.

CHAPTER NINE

April Fool's Day

Gunnery Sgt. Jack Coughlin, USMC

A SNIPER USUALLY SEES THE FACE OF HIS TARGET. ALTHOUGH THAT target may be a thousand yards away, with the scope on my rifle it is as if I can reach out and touch him with my fingertips. While targets look like human beings, they remain targets, and there is no personal attachment whatsoever. Feeling a personal kinship of any sort risks having second thoughts. So it came as a shock when I met someone I had shot not once, but twice, and had seen him fall. Normally that would mean that particular target was very dead. However, that was not the case with my friend, Achmed, the only man I ever shot who lived through the experience.

April 1 was the twelfth day of the war, and we launched our attack on Ad Diwaniyah, leaving the cloverleaf shortly after daylight, with the tanks in the lead and two companies of infantry fanning out in support. Despite all the noise we made, we still caught the Iraqis by surprise. Some of the enemy soldiers were still resting among the date palm groves in snug holes in which they had placed rugs and carpeting. Others were having breakfast in their mud huts, and we would later find warm food and cups of tea still on the tables, with canteens and helmets and weapons nearby. Just because our predecessor in the area, the 5th Marines, had not gone in after them, they thought they were safe from us, too.

Big Mistake. We were after the Bull.

When our tanks came highballing down the road, an Iraqi lookout jumped from his observation post and ran like hell to warn his friends,

175

but a flash of machine gun fire cut him down after just a few steps. In minutes, our artillery went psycho and rained explosives on the enemy positions. Tank cannons, TOW missiles, heavy machine guns, and that most lethal weapon of all, the Marine infantryman, joined the fight, and gunfire lit the dark, hazy sky of the early morning. The Marines tore through bunkers, trench lines and palm trees and shot any Iraqi soldier who tried to resist. As usual, the Fedayeen ran away before things got heavy.

I was again atop my truck, and after five minutes of scoping out the mud huts on the outskirts of the city, I spotted an enemy rifleman fighting from a foxhole exactly 286 meters to the south. Easy shot, so I smoke checked him, *bam*, and he was dead, his body twitching for a few more moments while his internal systems shut down. I noted the time, 7:47 am, on a green page of my sniper's log and got back to work. The place was noisy as a steel factory; the rocket-propelled grenades whooshed through the morning air and detonated on impact, and our tanks answered with volleys from their big man guns, heavy rounds that moved at a mile per second and seemed to lift the earth where they struck.

My second kill of the day was nothing less than a quick-draw showdown. We were taking Ad Diwaniyah block by block against bitter opposition, and the Panda drove us deeper into the urban area, bringing our Humvee to a halt near a group of Marines who were advancing through a cluster of huts. An Iraqi soldier suddenly appeared from between the two buildings right beside the road, his weapon at the ready with the butt stock to his shoulder and the barrel pointed slightly down. I had just gotten out of the truck and was in the same basic position. This was no faraway target but a man standing only about seventy-five yards away, point-blank range for my sniper rifle. He hesitated for a moment, perhaps startled by all of the Marines in the area, and then, too late, his eyes locked on mine. The brief flicker of uncertainty cost him his life. I killed him before he could get a shot off. In such situations, only an amateur dawdles. Professionals shoot.

As the front line advanced, the Panda moved us cautiously forward another few hundred yards to a bridge that curved to the right, arcing over another road that led to the besieged town. Our guys were already fighting at the other end of the span, and I was to help control this end and block any flanking movement.

I went back onto our Humvee and anchored myself into the now familiar solid prone shooting position to get a better look at a group of scruffy mud and cinder-block buildings that lined an area studded with palm trees. I slowly glassed the rooftops, doorways, windows, and alleys, the four places where death likes to hide in towns and cities.

The temperature was a mild seventy-eight degrees, but the rising sun had taken on its normal fierce brightness and bounced off the light-colored walls with such intensity that it was like staring into high-beam headlights.

Suddenly, three targets wearing green uniforms and carrying AK-47 rifles broke from cover and ran full speed from right to left. These were straight-up soldiers, not civilians, and I kept my scope on them as palm trees danced through my field of vision, blocking my view. The Bear did a laser range-check on the buildings where the men were heading: about 470 yards. A mirage shimmered from right to left, telling me a slight wind was moving across the battlefield and I fine-tuned an adjustment to compensate.

I had kept the crosshairs on them while dialing the scope, and when one paused at the corner of a building, at two minutes before ten o'clock in the morning, I put my crosshairs on his chest and squeezed the trigger. Targets rarely remain still in combat, however, and he moved at the last moment, spoiling a perfect shot. Instead of a center-mass hit, my bullet went through his throat, and the impact catapulted him back into the street.

Then came Achmed. I had just jacked another round into the chamber and was continuing to scan the area when he dashed from cover, running away but still carrying his rifle. I instantly fired a bullet in him. Somehow, perhaps just with forward momentum, he kept running, so I shot him again, and this time he went down and rolled out of view.

"I can't believe I missed," I told Panda.

"You didn't miss the second time, boss. I saw him go down," the Bear confirmed. I spent another ten minutes searching for the third soldier, who had vanished.

A little later, things quieted down and we got back into the Humvee and moved out, with me complaining the whole time. "I had the cross-hairs right on that sucker. I had him! How could he have kept going?" It was unsettling, and I knew that my fellow Marines would soon be riding me about it—"Coughlin missed!" McCoy would have a field day with this. It was a major fuckup.

We were taking a break back at the Main when a rogue RPG whooshed overhead, which was enough to convince Officer Bob that the headquarters was under attack. I yelled for him to calm down, but his frenzy startled one of the Amtrak machine gunners, who opened up with a full automatic burst and thoroughly killed a nearby donkey. I scrambled to get things back in order, and J-Matt Baker, the battalion XO, gave the donkey's bewildered owner some rations as payment.

Casey and I went forward again, and I found two of my snipers, Corporal Mark Evnin and Sergeant Dino Moreno, standing alongside Master Sergeant Bob Johnson from Bravo Tanks, studying the wrecked hulk of a civilian bus about a half mile to the northwest. Smoke oozed from the blown-out windows.

"Somebody's over there boss," Evnin told me. "Been getting some occasional fire. Maybe they're in the bus."

Top Johnson figured three Marine snipers were more than enough to handle whoever was in the bus, so he went back to his tanks, leaving us with a succinct instruction: "Kill 'em."

I climbed on the nearest Humvee and glassed the smoking carcass of the bus. For the first time in the war, I was working with fellow snipers, and we lapsed into the arcane sniper-spotter dialogue. Moreno was glassing an adjoining area, and Evnin acted as the spotter for both of us.

After three minutes of searching specific sectors, being patient and waiting for a mistake, I saw a shadow shift in the bus, and then the outline of a rifle appeared, an enemy sniper rising up for a shot. We had lased the bus at exactly 817 yards, more than eight football fields away.

"Mark," I said softly to Evnin, "I think I have movement in the bus, in the left third of the target zone."

Evnin swung his powerful scope around and responded, "I see the bus."

"Third of the way down, from the back to front, left side, fifth seat, window side."

"I see it."

"Does he have a weapon?" I asked for confirmation that I wasn't looking at a civilian.

"Sure does."

"What's the wind?"

"Three minutes left."

"Elevation?"

"Eight plus one." The conversation was brief, automatic, emotionless, professional. Moreno kept watch on the surrounding area, undistracted by our discovery.

I fine-tuned my scope to match Evnin's numbers. "OK. I'll hold an inch above center chest."

"Roger. On scope," Mark confirmed, holding his spotting scope steady on the bus. My spotter had the target.

"On target," I said. The shooter had the target, and everything was in place. I exhaled some breath and tightened on the trigger. I had this sucker as sure as if we were on the practice range. He was as good as dead anyway, for he might live through a meeting with one sniper, but not two, and never three.

"Fire when ready," Mark said.

My rifle barked and my shoulder took the recoil.

"Hit, center chest, target down," Evnin reported when the soldier was staggered by the big bullet and fell out of sight. Mark did not lower his scope. "Good shot, boss."

"Good windage," I told him. "Dead on." That was as high a compliment as one pro would give another. There were no high-fives or end zone celebrations, for we were professionals. We had done what we had been trained to do, so we expected both the cooperation and outcome. We switched back to assisting Moreno scan the rest of the area.

Inwardly, I was proud of Evnin. Mark was a stocky kid with brownish hair, an eager, happy-go-lucky youngster from Vermont who was hardcore into becoming a sniper. His talent level wasn't the best, because he had not yet finished sniper school when the war broke out, but he had worked so hard and had such an infectious enthusiasm that when my sniper/scout platoon went to Iraq, he came along with us. He would complete his training when we got back to the States, though it would be odd for a student to have kills to his credit before officially winning the title of sniper.

As it turned out, that was not to be. Within a few days, Mark Evnin would die in a firefight.

The battalion had finished with Ad Diwaniyah by lunchtime, having no casualties of our own but killing at least ninety-two Iraqi soldiers and taking another fifty-six as prisoners. The actual butcher's bill could have easily been three or four times what was reported, but we were intentionally lowballing the numbers, minimizing enemy casualties instead of maximizing them to avoid the Vietnam body-count habit that created unrealistic numbers and expectations.

Once again back at the Main I was gulping water and washing some of the thick dust off my skin when a Marine stopped by to tell me the security platoon had picked up some prisoners over in the area by the bridge, including a guy who had been hit by what appeared to be sniper rounds. The Panda and I headed for the prisoner pen and found the wounded man sitting on the ground with his legs crossed and plastic flexcuffs shackling his wrists.

He was no more than twenty years old, and his cheeks were bare, as if he were just starting to shave. He had taken one bullet in the left arm, and the second had penetrated his back and emerged out the top of his left breast. Somehow the slug went through without ripping out his heart or hitting anything major. He was not even bleeding hard.

I checked the wounds, and they looked about the right size. Was this the guy I had shot? I grabbed a nearby interpreter and asked the boy how long he had been wounded. The Iraqi refused to talk, and his dark eyes flashed in anger, but I saw some fright, too. I put on my war face, leaned close to let my own eyes pierce his, shouted a few choice expletives, and then had the interpreter ask again. The kid was growing pale, and this time he answered, saying he had been trying to surrender when he was shot. Bullshit. He still had on his boots and had been carrying a rifle while he was running. "Where?" I wanted to know, and he described the same area. Same place.

He said the first bullet hit his left arm and sent him stumbling forward, off balance. Then another shot went through his shoulder. I asked why, if he wanted to give up, he didn't throw down his rifle and take off his boots. He said if he tried to do that, his own people would have killed him. I decide to ease up on him. I had the interpreter tell the prisoner that I was the one who had shot him. The Iraqi soldier glanced at my bug M40A1 rifle and nodded.

Weird, conflicting emotions swept over me. I was glad that I had not missed a target, but I was also strangely delighted that this guy had survived. Never had I felt personal responsibility for the safety of an enemy combatant, so this sudden kinship was unexpected, and it was kind of cool.

The fighting was over for the day, so I didn't want him to die. I felt he had earned a new lease on life. I called him "Achmed" because I didn't know his real name. By doing so, I crossed the invisible line of humanizing my enemy.

Next, I had Achmed carried to the front of a long line of other wounded Iraqi soldiers at an aid station, and I told the doctor, an old friend, to patch him up. "He's the only one I've ever shot that lived through the experience," I said, and the doc balked.

He apparently thought that I wanted to make sure the kid didn't survive much longer in order to keep my record intact. No, I explained, just the opposite. This new patient was one lucky bastard, so I wanted him to receive special treatment. The interpreter explained to the soldier, "You're hooked up man. You're a celebrity."

He began to lose that defiant look. As the doctor removed the shirt, pumped in some anesthetic, and started to work, I stood there, talking quietly to the boy.

GAS . . . Gas . . . Gas . . . !!

The dreaded warning roared through the area in a hasty echo of shouts, and Marines dropped whatever they were doing to put on their gas masks. Achmed, flat on his back but not unconscious, grew frightened when we covered our heads with the big hoods and goggles, and we must have looked to him like a bunch of unworldly, blunt-nosed elephants. I called out to the Panda, my words muffled, to bring me one of the masks we had taken off some dead Iraqi officers earlier in the day. He was back in moments and tossed me the mask; I worked it over Achmed's face, seeing a look of pure gratitude. The other wounded Iraqis had no protection.

I removed the mask when the "All Clear" was given after the false alarm. When the doctor finished working, the kid was moved to a cot. I knelt beside him and had the interpreter explain that he was going to be all right and that I would be back to see him later and bring him some food. He was woozy but never took his eyes off of me.

I went back to work at the Main for a while, then grabbed some coffee and rations and returned to the prisoner aid station. Achmed was gone, having been taken off by the military police to another prisoner cage in the rear, so I tossed aside the MRE rations and dined instead on fried Spam with my friends. It was disappointing, but it was war.

After chow I was briefed on where we were going the next day, cleaned my weapons, and settled in to get some sleep on another cold night in Iraq, banishing Achmed from my mind. He was a onetime thing, and while I was glad he survived, my job was not to coddle enemy soldiers but to kill them. If we ever faced each other again on the battlefield, I would shoot him again without hesitation.

I now had ten kills in Iraq. Then there was Achmed, who was blessed and protected by his merciful Allah. Should have been eleven, but things had not been going quite right all day.

Earlier, I almost got my foot shot off by accident, and Casey almost committed suicide by RPG.

Gunny Don Houston and I were on patrol along a canal when a gunshot snapped out. The round impacted right at my feet, punching up a small column of dirt an inch from my boot.

"Oops," said Houston.

"Oops?" I yelled at my buddy. "What the fuck do you mean, *oops?*"

"OK. Oops, sorry."

That broke the tension, and I cracked a smile. He had accidently pulled the trigger on his rifle, but it had been pointed at the ground. I told him to forget it—after all, shit happens in war—but I came out of the incident knowing that I was one lucky sumbitch.

Meanwhile, Casey and some of the boys had cleaned out a bunker in which they had found a cache of AK-47s, machine guns, plastique explosives, and about fifty rocket-propelled grenades, enough to arm a whole platoon. They stacked the weapons and set about destroying them with a thermite grenade, a big-league weapon that generates as much heat as a welding torch and melts through anything. Casey unwrapped the grenade, then handed it over to a sergeant who wanted to toss it.

They jogged away when the grenade was thrown, and we heard the quiet pop as the little bomb ignited and began to sizzle through the stacked weapons. Then came a loud BANG and a WHOOSH, and an RPG flew past Casey's ear and thudded into a nearby sand berm. The intense heat of the thermite grenade was cooking off the pile of live ammo. Casey and the sergeant crawled back behind a little mound some farmer had built and hunkered down while more rocket-propelled grenades came to life and went flying. For the next five minutes, the aimless rain of RPGs zoomed about, giving the place the look of a major counterattack—or a carnival. Everyone chewed dirt. Luckily, an RPG must be manually armed in order to detonate on impact, so the actual damage was light.

"Were you really trying to shell your own troops?" I asked the unusually sheepish Casey as he was dusting off.

He gave the only appropriate response, "Fuck you." The lieutenant had just endured another embarrassing lesson about how, in combat, even doing the right thing can go wrong.

Achmed, the murdered donkey, a bullet that almost took off my foot, and Casey's attack on the rest of us made a weird kind of sense later that evening, when I realized that we had been fighting on April Fool's Day.

CHAPTER TEN

The Nastiest Fight

Gina Cavallaro and Matt Larsen

BY THE TIME OF THE BIG FIREFIGHT, SGT. ADAM PEEPLES HAD ALREADY killed plenty of men—bomb planters, getaway drivers, militiamen, and others who openly tried to kill first.

But until that chilly winter night in western Iraq, when so many lethal projectiles were flying through the air that "it looked like the Fourth of July," he said, he hadn't killed an enemy sniper.

It happened on the third night of a major offensive against a slithering nest of Al Qaeda fighters who, for some time, had been lording over the densely populated Ma'Laab district of eastern Ramadi and operating almost undisturbed. They were ruthlessly killing Americans and Iraqis, helping to uphold Ramadi's reputation as one of the most dangerous places for U.S. troops in Iraq.

The city of about a half million people is on the main route between Syria and Baghdad, and from the start of U.S. operations in Iraq in March 2003, it was rife with violence as Al Qaeda fought to establish and maintain its stronghold there.

But this operation would be the beginning of the end for Al Qaeda in Ramadi. It was about to get rudely routed from its cozy urban hideaway by hundreds of dismounted U.S. and Iraqi soldiers backed by the firepower of M1 Abrams tanks, Bradley fighting vehicles, and AH-64 Apache attack helicopters.

As the February 2007 operation was launched, Peeples and seven other men took over a three-story house in the neighboring Askan district at the western edge of the Ma'Laab district, where a giant Texas barrier or T-wall was going to be erected to seal off travel routes between the two adjoining districts.

Two nights earlier, the squad had lost a soldier, Spc. Louis G. Kim, to what Peeples called "a lucky shot" by a machine gunner in a window. So instead of infiltrating the area and entering the selected house on this night through the front door, the team rode in a tracked Brad and climbed through a jagged hole busted open by the vehicle and its 25 mm gun in the side of the house.

What started for the team as a nighttime over-watch mission to catch stragglers slipping through the house-to-house search and to stop Al Qaeda reinforcements from migrating into the fight from Askan ended up as a textbook urban battle—a rooftop-to-rooftop firefight across a ramshackle concrete cityscape that raged almost nonstop over the six hours it took for dawn to arrive.

On the rooftop of the house they had taken over, with the home's occupants cowering in fear one floor below as the team's medic kept an eye on them, the soldiers hunkered low behind a four-foot wall that lined the edge of the roof, dodging hot green tracers that split the cool night air over their heads.

In the first couple of hours, between bursts of enemy fire, the American soldiers fired back with their own bursts—taking cover, then popping up, aiming, and firing before ducking back down again.

The team had what it thought was plenty of firepower. Peeples and his partner, Spc. Craig Stout, had their sniper gear, and the squad members with them had a 240B machine gun, M203 40 mm grenade launchers, an M249 squad automatic weapon, hand grenades, and AT4s. But the gunfire was unrelenting and chaotic, and eventually they had to be resupplied.

The men took positions all around the rooftop and took turns firing and reloading.

"You could hear bullets whizzing by; they were hitting the wall we were hiding behind," said Stout, who was on his first deployment and had been trained as a sniper by his battalion. "It was massive amounts of shooting, but you kind of have the attitude that you're invincible and they're not going to hit you. We would just lay down. I would even stop and smoke a cigarette in the middle of all of it, and I could see the bullets flying over my head."

In fact, no one was hit, and a second over-watch team to the east of their location saw no action at all.

Even with the advantage of night vision goggles and PEQ-2 infrared lasers on their rifles, the men said, they couldn't easily make out the enemy human shapes in the night, only their telltale muzzle flashes, which were coming from rooftops and windows all around. The soldiers tried to shoot the enemy combatants as they saw them run past, like players at a shooting gallery on a summer boardwalk.

"You could see people running across windows and rooftops and jumping roof to roof and over walls. They were running right in front of us in this alley. We had to throw grenades down there because they were coming closer and they were trying to flank us," Stout said.

Stout was using his PEQ to guide the 240B machine gunner onto targets, but everyone had resorted to just aiming at the muzzle flashes.

"I had a universal night sight on there in front of my scope and it was, 'Find the muzzle flash, put two rounds on it, and shift to the next one.' You couldn't see the people, you know," Peeples said.

As the fighting became more and more fierce, the Americans could hear the gunfire getting closer as the enemy gunmen who weren't wounded or dead boldly hopscotched toward them over the walled, flat rooftops and through ground-level courtyards, avoiding the roadways they knew would bring certain death. The two Bradleys parked with their 25 mm guns aimed down the streets that were the enemy's natural migration routes might have had something to do with that.

"There was a courtyard wall that they would have had to scale to get to us, and we had that covered. They never had a hope of getting into our position because there was a north-south running road that divided us from them, and that gave us some standoff," Peeples said.

Precision shooting and grenades kept the most determined insurgents from getting too close. "The guys who came close got killed. Everybody on that roof killed several guys," he said.

Peeples is more than six feet tall, a blond country boy from Griffin, Georgia, who got a BB gun when he was five, started duck hunting when he was seven, and killed his first deer when he was nine. He set out to join the Marine Corps one day in 2002, but an Army recruiter won him over when he caught him first in the hallway. Sniping wasn't a job that Peeples was aware of at the time, but he knew he wanted to be an infantryman.

"I knew going to Iraq was a possibility, and it was something I wanted to do. It was sort of a 'prove yourself' kind of thing, you know?"

On his first deployment to Iraq in February 2004, he was in Samarra with a line company in First Battalion, Twenty-sixth Infantry, Second Brigade Combat Team, First Infantry Division out of Schweinfurt, Germany, the same unit he would deploy to Ramadi with in 2006.

"I did every job you could do in an infantry platoon," Peeples said, remembering his life as a grunt and how impressed he had been with the snipers he got to observe when he helped provide security at a Special Forces team house. It was a whole new world to see soldiers working in a small team with the freedom to ply a craft of precision.

While he was with them, he saw a couple of big fights. "They were right there beside us and it was really impressive watching them work," he said. "They're professional and it's all about finding a target, taking the target out, and moving on to the next one. Those two guys up in a bunker did more damage than the whole platoon."

Before that gig in Samarra, he said, he hadn't even thought about sniping, and now he laughs when asked whether he thought he would die that night three years later in Ramadi as the wild rooftop ride unfolded. Pushing the thought aside with a dismissive "no," he recalled a couple of close calls during the Ramadi battle when some of the enemy fighters came within twenty-five meters of their position and tried to close with them.

The bad guys were so close at one point, the American soldiers could hear them shouting and screaming. The Americans shouted and screamed back. "They were yelling 'Allah akbar,' and we're yelling, 'Fuck you!' and other things you can imagine," Peeples said, "and we could hear them pulling out their wounded, you could hear them screaming. It's a unique sound."

The voices and sounds became an audio map that helped the soldiers gauge their enemy's distance and distinguish their communications by the pitch of those sounds.

"We could tell what they were doing by listening to their voices; some sounded like commands. I don't think the majority of them knew where we were at. They could see our muzzle flashes, but anyone who exposed themselves pretty much got shot," he said.

Describing the engagement as "the nastiest fight I've ever seen," Peeples thinks he might have played an early role in kicking off that fight when he and his team took their position in the Askan district, on the other side of where the blocking wall was to go up.

Peeples believed that many of the Al Qaeda fighters used that district to stage their attacks and the U.S. soldiers could engage them on that side before they infiltrated the Ma'Laab district. His hunch was confirmed almost immediately.

It was late at night, and the main operation had already begun on the ground in the Ma'Laab district. After busting into the house and climbing to the rooftop through an inside stairway, the men began quietly surveying their surroundings. Peeples peered into an alleyway and what he saw through his infrared laser pointer was a fraction of what awaited. What happened next unleashed the heavy metal they would fight for the next six hours.

"I look down and there's two guys right below me not even ten yards away, directly below me and they're both on a knee and they're just whispering," Peeples said. "I had my infrared laser PEQ-2 on my rifle, came over the top, put half a mag into them, and that was it. As soon as I did that, the whole horizon lit up. We just took an unbelievable amount of fire."

On the rooftop with Peeples and Stout was Staff Sgt. Coy Tinsley, the squad leader for the rest of the security team and a soldier Peeples had befriended on their first deployment together to Samarra.

"On my first tour, I think it was just a bunch of uneducated guys who would shoot an RPG just to make some money without thinking about the repercussions," said Tinsley explaining the quality of the enemy fighter he encountered in Iraq.

At the start of U.S. operations in Iraq in March 2003, one of the earliest decisions of the Coalition Provisional Authority—to disband the Iraqi army—left tens of thousands of former soldiers suddenly unemployed and with no way to provide for their families. A rapidly growing and influential Al Qaeda in Iraq quickly capitalized on the misery and resentment of these soldiers by offering them a quick way to make a buck by attacking U.S. forces.

But by the time Peeples and Tinsley were in Ramadi two years later, Iraq had become the place to go to fight Americans, and the dumb insurgents had already been killed. Killing Americans was a wholesale business, and the war was in full bloom.

"These guys were seasoned fighters, the way they moved. They had more of a fighting discipline," Tinsley said.

During the rooftop firefight, the heaviest contact they were taking, he said, was coming from the south and southwest of their position. Feeling besieged and potentially outmanned, the team decided to call in air support after identifying several houses where there was a lot of activity.

"There were periods of calm, and it would start up again. After we dropped the big bomb, it pretty much calmed down," Tinsley said, referring to a five-hundred-pound bomb they called in on a house about one hundred meters away.

Over the hours, with some new lulls in the fighting, they were resupplied by the Bradley crew that had dropped them off at the beginning of the operation, one of the advantages of being mechanized infantrymen, Peeples said. "They brought in a bunch of preloaded mags ready to go. They brought us a crate of grenades, a bunch of 240 ammo, three AT4s, and the fight just kept on going. You have your lulls of five or ten minutes, and then it would just kick off again."

During one of these lulls, Peeples took the time to scan a building about seventy-five meters away that he believed was the source of a spate of gunshots that were more accurate than most.

"It had started easing off a little bit. We had called in three [guided missile launch rockets] and a five-hundred-pound bomb, and we'd shot three AT4s, so the buildings were pretty devastated. But there were still guys creeping around up there, and we were taking potshots over our heads," Peeples said.

Listening closely to the shots, Peeples figured that there was at least one shooter who was probably using something like an SVD Dragunov sniper rifle. "A couple of shots hit the wall, and I said, 'This is a sniper . . . or he thinks he is anyway,'" he said.

During the fighting Peeples took the universal night sight off the front of his rifle because, at more than a pound in weight, it started to get heavy and he wasn't really using it to find targets that were giving themselves away with muzzle flashes. But he put the sight back on to scan the building he suspected of being a hideout.

Peeples used a customized weapon he built with $2,500 of his own money and parts he mail-ordered from the United States. Using the Army-issued lower receiver of his M16, the part that houses the trigger mechanism and has the serial number on it, he added a twenty-inch match grade Olympic Arms barrel and the Olympic Arms free floated hand guard; a JP Rifles adjustable gas block; a Vortex flash suppressor; an Olympic Arms match grade upper receiver; an ACE skeleton stock; and a cyclic rate reducing buffer spring assembly; and finished it with the Packmire pistol grip that he likes.

"It was an extremely accurate weapon, every bit as accurate as the M24 was. But I went to that length because when you get a chance to get a shot, you don't want your equipment to fail you, you want it to be better than you are. If I had a good shot on a dude's head and I were to miss because the rifle's not good enough to make the shot, then why take the shot?" he said.

With the sweat cooling on the skin of his bare forearms, Peeples propped his weapon up on the wall using his PEQ-2 and with his right eye on the scope went slowly from window to window, using his floodlight setting to look into the rooms through open windows and doors. The PEQ-2 is an infrared laser illuminator with two settings. A broad floodlight for illuminating an area and a narrow stream designed as an aiming device. The infrared light can only be seen with the aid of night observation devices.

It had been a couple of hours since the heavy fighting ended, and the other men, in a relatively relaxed mode for the moment, turned part of their attention to what Peeples was doing. "It was kind of an exciting thing that he did, so we were all looking at him," Stout said.

The night was clear, and the air smelled like gunpowder. Peeples didn't have his finger on the trigger because he didn't expect to see anybody. As he passed over one of the open windows, however, a brief but telling glint caught his trained eye—and he went back to it. This time he switched his PEQ-2 to the narrow setting.

"It went into the back wall, which was white, and the splatter from the laser just lit him up in silhouette. I could see the guy. He had a table set up and a chair, and he had something that he had his rifle sitting on like a pillow or a blanket or sack of sand or something," Peeples said. "I could clearly see a rifle and a guy sitting down. I could tell his weapon had a scope on it."

When Peeples finished his second deployment, he said, his NCO evaluation report listed him as having killed forty-three enemy combatants during his time as a sniper. But nothing compared to the thrill of snaring another sniper, an experience few can boast of.

"It's kind of cool when you can see someone and you know they can't see you. He was close. I could see him back there trying to figure out where to shoot at and where to see us. I can imagine from the shots he's taking at us he couldn't see. It was not accurate fire."

The distance between them was shorter than a football field, and Peeples didn't hesitate.

"From the time I saw him to the time I shot him was six or seven seconds," he said. "It was a head shot, just dropped him. He just fell right on top of his rifle and knocked the table over." Peeples conceded that, even though the enemy sniper's shots weren't accurate enough to kill him or any of his men because he lacked the technological advantages of night vision and laser aiming devices, "he had an idea of what he was doing" and would have been a serious threat had he lived until daylight.

That night was Peeples's chance to take out one of an unknown number of snipers operating in Al Anbar province.

A spate of other bizarre incidents took place within three days of the operation, Peeples recalled, like the time he spotted about eight men, all wearing purple-and-white Adidas warm-up suits, openly preparing to emplace 155mm artillery shells into a roadway in broad daylight.

Incredulous, he watched as they breached the concertina wire set up on each side of the road, and he tried to call for air fire so he wouldn't have to give his position away. But when he radioed for help, he was told the helicopters were busy so he took matters into his own hands.

Peeples had a whole squad with him at the hide site, and he instructed the 240B machine gunners to set up on the guy carrying the shells so that when he initiated the attack with a single shot at the guy who was the clear ringleader, the others could open up quickly.

"With eight guys in front of you," he said, "you don't want to kill one, you want to kill all of them. I shot the first guy right in the chest, he was about one hundred yards away, and dropped him."

Immediately, one of the 240B machine gunners, whose barrel was poking through a small loophole, pushed through the crappy masonry in the wall and opened up on the group through a bigger hole, as did the 203s.

"The guy that was carrying one of the 155s dropped it, and he was trying to come back out and grab it for some reason so I shot him and dropped him on the spot," Peeples said.

Four were killed, the rest got away, but the action turned into a forty-five-minute firefight with other insurgents hidden in adjacent buildings who popped onto the scene like Clapper lightbulbs, seemingly activated by the sound of gunfire. It wasn't long before backup arrived, though, as Peeples had called a quick reaction force before he took his first shot, and it rolled out the gate toward them about three minutes after the shooting began.

"This dude came out of a roof access door, I shot him. Then right below him a guy popped out of a window and one of the Bradleys blew the guy out of the window, and what was left of him was hanging by a leg from a telephone wire," Peeples said.

As bullets pinged all around, one of them zipped through the metal casing of a window he was shooting out of. The brass casing from the round caught Peeples in the face and leg and hit his friend and partner Sgt. Matt Thompson in the hand, leg, and face.

"It felt a lot worse than it was. We were like, 'damn,' and we stepped back from the window. We were both fine, but there was a lot of blood," Peeples said.

As soon as the firing started to die down, he said, the Brads came up, dropped ramp on the concertina wire, and the squad piled in on top of four guys who were already in the troop compartment, which seats five.

On the way in, Thompson got hung up on the wire as the ramp was going up. As it was lowered again to give him a chance to get unhooked, Peeples started to reach out for him when "this dude pops out about 150 yards away and is getting ready to line us both up and the Brad decimated him right there. We got out of there."

In another incident a day later, Thompson and Peeples were in a hide site before a planned operation. The building was adjacent to another site known as OP Hotel, where another team was holed up. But OP Hotel didn't have the bird's-eye view that Peeples and Thompson had down a north-south route, and while they scanned down that road from their site, they saw something that made their jaws drop.

"Holy shit, there were like thirty-plus armed guys on this road, and they were moving tactically in a file, and there were a squad or two crossing the road," Peeples said. It was the first time he'd ever seen a military formation in Iraq.

"One guy pulled security and one guy ran across pulling security, and this threw me off," he said. "There was actually like a big gathering of them, like twenty of them standing around smoking with RPGs on their backs and just chilling, because they knew nobody from OP Hotel could see them. They didn't know we were there," he said.

The men weren't uniformed, but to be on the safe side, Peeples called back to the tactical operations center to ask if there were "friendlies" to the south of their position they might be unaware of, like Iraqi armed forces.

The answer came back "negative," and Peeples also learned that no attack helicopters were available. So he and his team lit up the group, just pummeled it with all they had.

"We unleashed and, I mean, it was just, I mean it was ugly. The guys that we didn't kill on our street squirted onto the east-west streets and the Bradleys got them. I talked to the guy in the battalion TOC who was doing the [unmanned aerial vehicle] feed, and he said he was flying over and said he just saw bodies all over the roads," Peeples said. "None of them got a shot off, there was probably less than one magazine from an AK that got shot. There were like twenty-five or thirty KIAs."

In their first mission as snipers in Ramadi in December 2006, Peeples and Stout moved into a hide site late one night where they could get eyes on an intersection that was about one hundred meters away. The intersection seemed to blow up under every U.S. vehicle that crossed it, and because it was a main travel route, the snipers were given a chance to put some rounds into anyone messing around with it.

The next afternoon, Peeples said, "I was using a tactical periscope to observe around the mounds." It was cold and windy outside, and when you're sitting in an abandoned building just waiting for something to happen, you get cold. Peeples and the nine men he brought with him were in their sleeping bags trying to shield themselves from the wind. They took turns watching the objective.

"Right at the intersection there was a dude, about a fourteen-year-old kid, with a screwdriver and he was just hacking away at the road. So I zoomed in on my periscope, and he had a blasting cap in one hand. It wasn't asphalt, it was like a hard-packed dirt. He actually had an IED already in there, and he was just trying to get the blasting cap into it so he could run the wire," Peeples said.

Stout fired, hit the teenager in the right neck and chest area, and watched him drop and roll right off the side into a ditch. As if on cue, two other teens they hadn't seen popped out, ran, and jumped into a car.

"They were speeding off, and we're shooting up the car on the way out," Peeples said.

It was critical that the team's first command-sanctioned mission go well, and it had. Peeples and his team did their job and successfully eliminated at least one IED emplacer.

His first experience with an enemy sniper, though, happened before any of his other fights in Ramadi and would end up being one that claimed the life of a U.S. soldier. Peeples was afraid of how his outlook on the soldier's death might sound, but he said it anyway. "I don't mean this in a bad way, but that guy right there saved a lot of our guys' lives," Peeples said of Staff Sgt. Christopher Swanson, who died on July 22, 2006, with only a few days to go before redeployment after a year in country.

It happened during a daytime patrol in the Tameem area of Ramadi on what the Army calls a right-seat/left-seat ride in the days before an area of operation is handed over to the next unit. In this case, Swanson's platoon in Bravo Company, Second Battalion, Sixth Infantry, First Brigade, First Armored Division was leading the way on a combat patrol in which no contact with the enemy had been made as they moved through the area.

As Peeples remembers it, "We're getting ready to go and a squad had moved up to a roof to cover our movement. A guy had knocked out a loophole in the wall up there so he could look through and not expose his head. Swanson looked through it and got shot right through that loophole. That was their last mission, and they took a KIA on that mission from a sniper."

The death, he said, was a tragic jolt to everyone and an eye-opener for him and the soldiers around him, many of whom had deployed together to Samarra where they hadn't encountered a sniper threat.

Like the sniper Peeples would later kill, the one who killed Swanson acted like a trained professional. "The guy who shot the kid on the patrol knew what he was doing. He tracked our movement through sector and knew exactly where to set up on us so he could take a shot. He knew we'd take one of three buildings and set up his shot. He knew about the loophole," Peeples said.

He professed to having learned little about enemy snipers while he was in Iraq, only that he'd heard they would be recruited off the street and given air rifles as a start. But, as with other U.S. snipers, Peeples had also heard that Chechen-trained enemy snipers were in Iraq, and while he was on duty as a sniper, he thinks he may have had another encounter with Swanson's killer.

"He shot an IR beacon off the windowsill from about 150 meters away. He thought it was one of our Kpots I guess. He operated pretty much solely. He killed several Iraqi army guys, and a second lieutenant was shot on a run between two buildings; he was shot through the meat of the shoulder," Peeples said.

He wanted to find the guy, he said, but "I knew that there wasn't really any way that I could go out and try to find him. He's targeting guys he knows are there. He's looking for coalition forces. The reason he's there is because he's looking for coalition forces."

Besides, he said, Ramadi at that time was a target-rich environment populated by insurgents who made themselves more readily visible, sometimes in large numbers, by planting improvised explosive devices in plain view, day and night.

"A sniper's job is to kill the enemy. Bottom line is, that's what you're there to do. Shooting one bullet and killing one guy is great, but when you got eight guys in front of you, you need to come up with some other kind of plan. That's what we did, we did ambushes. Nothing fancy like taking these long one-shots or anything like that. If there was a fight, the commander wanted us up front, and that's where I wanted to be, too," Peeples said.

CHAPTER ELEVEN

Storm Clouds Gather over Go Noi Island

John J. Culberston

A TALL, LEAN, AND SERIOUS PROFESSIONAL, JERRY DOHERTY HAD A RARE combination of courage and compassion tempered by considerable combat experience. He had commanded Hotel Company for the first time in the spring of 1966, in the offensives around Chu Lai and Tam Ky. After his tour of three months on the DMZ as battalion logistics officer, he'd volunteered to guide Hotel Company's battered seasoned grunts once again in the Winter Offensive of 1967. The Third Marine Amphibious Force Command planned a series of thrusts aimed at dislodging the indigenous Viet Cong main force units that controlled the rice basin north of the new 5th Marine combat base at An Hoa.

As a preliminary action, Lieutenant Colonel W. C. Airheart, commander of the 2nd Battalion, 5th Marines, ordered Captain Doherty and the other line commanders to lead extensive regular patrols into the rice basin north of An Hoa. This area was to become infamous during 1967 as the staging area for some twenty-one enemy battalions. The Viet Cong used the An Hoa Basin to replenish their supplies of rice and munitions prior to pushing south to continue the Communist military onslaught on Saigon.

Captain Doherty personally led his Marines through the rice paddies to search out and destroy the enemy combat units that harassed the civilian agrarian Vietnamese population. The Communists even murdered the village chiefs and teachers, doctors, and merchants, who showed any deference or cooperation toward American efforts to pacify the country-side. Doherty was above all things a realist, and he maintained a strong dependence on common sense and rational thought. After a series of patrols where the grunts of Hotel Company were ambushed after search-ing villages, the Hotel skipper had been ordered to utilize ARVN officers as advisors. Doherty got the hunch that wouldn't go away: Perhaps his ARVN friends weren't so loyal to the American war effort as the senior U.S. generals and their staff planners thought. As a result, on the next major sweep Doherty wisely left the ARVN soldiers behind at An Hoa, and glory be—there was no surprise ambush! After that incident Jerry Doherty relied on his own good judgment and looked after his own troops personally.

Sergeant Tom Casey was surrounded by officers of the 2nd Battal-ion, 5th Marine line companies as Colonel Airheart carefully went over his operation plan. It called for a battalion-size assault into the Deadly Arizona Territory, which was tentatively scheduled to jump off on Janu-ary 24, 1967. Airheart addressed the assembled leaders of Echo, Foxtrot, Golf, and Hotel Companies, represented by their company command-ers, platoon commanders, and company gunnery sergeants. Tom Casey would receive the marching orders for his sniper units, which would be OPCON (under operational control) of the rifle company commanders.

Colonel Airheart glanced up from the crude desk in his hooch, lit by a pair of naked lightbulbs with green shades suspended from the rafters. He looked at Jerry Doherty and George Burgett, his two most seasoned combat leaders. Doherty and Burgett had come over with 2/5 from Okinawa in 1966. After the brutal and heartbreaking combat along the DMZ at Con Thein that summer, both young captains were becoming short-timers and scheduled to return home within a few months. As a sergeant, Colonel Airheart had fought the desperate Japanese in World War II in the Pacific on some of the bloodiest island campaigns. He became a captain and combat leader years later in Korea during savage fighting, and his Marines were forged into outstanding fighters in the icy blizzards and rugged mountains. Airheart meant to put his veteran cold-hearted killers to work immediately. Communist military activity had grown by degrees in the An Hoa Basin, until almost every patrol or company-size sweep was ambushed in force and taken on in vicious, close-quarter firefights that tested the Marines to the maximum.

A man of action, the colonel had determined to strike with force directly into the Viet Cong's riverine sanctuary along with converging meanders of the Vu Gia and Thu Bon rivers in the Arizona Territory. Airheart had planned to send Foxtrot and Golf Companies, reinforced by Headquarters and Service Companies, which would provide 81mm mortar support and handle medevac and most signals operations. Captain Doherty's Hotel Company was perhaps the most seasoned veteran company in the battalion, but they had been constantly patrolling off the firebase at Phu Loc 6 for the last few weeks and needed rest. However, at the last minute Airheart changed his plans.

"Jerry, I know your Marines have run the paddies hard the last few weeks," he said to Doherty. "The brass has ordered a full-scale attack of Go Noi Island next week. This operation will be planned and implemented at the battalion level. You realize that the future reputation of the battalion as well as my own career depends on the successful total destruction of the Viet Cong main forces and their North Vietnamese advisors.

"Intelligence advises us that the R-20th Main Force Regiment is occupying Go Noi Island and launching harassment and interdiction operations against our patrols along the river. Intelligence further estimates that a full-strength Viet Cong main force division is operating in the area and receiving tactical aid and leadership from a company-size North Vietnamese advisory unit that is active in their combat planning and operational decisions. I feel I have no choice but to order Hotel Company to take the field again and spearhead the battalion into attack."

Jerry Doherty had seen enough combat during two full tours of command. He had learned to place the security of his company and the lives of his Marine brothers ahead of his personal opportunities for combat distinction. As for the men of Hotel Company—they had a deep and abiding faith that their commander would do his utmost to see that they lived to see tomorrow.

Captain Doherty looked as lean as Abe Lincoln as he leaned over Colonel Airheart's desk and spoke slowly. "My men have run their legs off," he said. "It's our turn to guard the airstrip after coming off Phu Loc 6 and constant patrolling in the Arizona. I appreciate the honor of leading the operation, but my men are worn pretty thin, plus my best platoon commander, Jim Kirschke, has been crippled by that freak explosive device last week. Colonel, I don't know if we'd do the job you're expecting us to do! Lieutenant Kirschke is my right hand, and we don't have a seasoned replacement."

"Jerry, you and George Burgett are going to take your companies into Go Noi reinforced with extra corpsmen, S-2 scouts, K-P dogs and their handlers, and Sergeant Casey's sniper teams," Airheart replied. "Sergeant Casey's boys have killed over sixty Viet Cong already at Chu Lai and off Phu Loc 6. We'll have the 1st Marine Aircraft Wing on standby, with F-4s loaded with napalm. The artillery batteries of the 11th Marines here at An Hoa will be ready to support your attack. Hell, all we have to do now is rest the troops a couple days and go kick Charlie's ass off that island and into the river. Jerry, you and George are my fighters! I wouldn't send you if I wasn't certain you could kick the shit out of these Viet Cong infiltrators. The Arizona Territory and the An Hoa Basin belong to the United States Marine Corps. By god, I'm ordering you to carry a message to our neighbors that Mother Green is serving their eviction notice."

Captain Doherty looked at his close friend, Captain George Burgett, and just shook his head, knowing further argument was a waste of effort. It would be just like up on the DMZ in 1966 again. Foxtrot and Hotel. Slaughter alley. Find the VC. Fire their sorry asses up. Bring up the heavy guns. Call in fast movers heavy-laden with tanks of napalm-jelly-gasoline-death under their wings. Watch your men, your brothers, your sons, loaded like cordwood into the Sea Knights. March back to base with tears streaming down your cheeks. Enter the hooches and count the empty cots. Remember the faces of your boys. Nineteen. Twenty. Cut down in their prime in a war no one understood. A war no one was allowed to win. Wake up late in the darkness of a sweat-laced night, picture the faces of your Marines, and realize that part of you has died with them.

Captain Doherty and George Burgett saluted Colonel Airheart and left the duty hut knowing they would have to face the bullets again and write the letters to the parents after the battle: "Your son Thomas was a brave Marine. He willingly sacrificed his life for his friends on . . ." Anyone who thought being a combat leader didn't have a downside was smoking something strange. No amount of medals or heroic honors could outweigh the personal sense of responsibility and grief that plagued even the most successful Marine officers. Personally I was proud to serve with Captain Doherty and be one of his deadliest riflemen. Then again, I couldn't even begin to comprehend the psychological and moral effects of our actions until I grew much older.

Sergeant Casey, on the other hand, was a true combat Marine. He believed that it was his solemn duty as an American to crush the ugly specter of Communism wherever it reared its ugly head. Casey would be sending three sniper teams into harm's way on Operation Tuscaloosa. Ron Willoughby and Vaughn Nickell would team up with Ulysses Black and Loren Kleppe and be attached to Hotel Company. Jim Flynn and Denny Toncar would be attached to Headquarters Company. Sergeant Casey was ordered to man the radio at the battalion communications center where Colonel Airheart and his staff would monitor the maneuvering companies' progress as they crossed the river and went into the assault.

On January 24 the three sniper teams left An Hoa with Hotel and Headquarters and Service Companies, while Foxtrot filed off the west slope of Phu Loc 6 to join Hotel later that afternoon, when both companies would approach the river from the south. The snipers knew their main responsibility was to screen the grunts' front as they went into the attack. However, if any opportunities to shoot enemy patrols or break up a Viet Cong ambush presented themselves, the snipers would be ready for action. Ron Willoughby watched the red mud squish and cake around the leather uppers of his jungle boots. The sky was swollen with moisture, and gray clouds slowly scudded across low-lying hills, threatening rain. Willoughby always kept a green towel draped over the scopes of his M1-D sniper rifle. Vaughn Nickell followed Willoughby's footprints, ever mindful of the need to watch out for mines and booby traps. Both Willoughby and Nickell had seen other point scouts with the grunt patrols trip explosive devices and get wounded by shrapnel, or even worse—get blown up by a command-detonated bomb or mortar round rigged with a fuse and electric wire. Some point scouts were instantly torn apart by the blasts, while others lived to tell their tales, showing off the tears and jagged lumps inside their wounds that still carried pieces of fractured steel.

The Hotel point scouts were reputed to be some of the finest in the 1st Marine Division and had earned their spurs along countess trails from Chu Lai to the DMZ during the summer of 1966. Willoughby watched John Lafley lead the column with a smooth gait and decisive judgment born of countless hours patrolling the heavily booby-trapped and mined jungle. John Lafley, part Salish Indian from the wilds of Montana, was Hotel's chief point scout and master of the "approach march." Today he was ushering a new apprentice, who walked "trace" or second position in the column. Lafley stopped periodically, and pointed out earthen mounds, depressions, thickets, and cuts in the terrain that could harbor mines or an enemy sniper team poised to "fire up" the Marine column and then escape like drifting smoke into their spider holes.

PFC John Culbertson paid a hell of a lot more attention to Lance Corporal Lafley than he had at Oklahoma University, where he'd screwed off, drinking and carousing late with his buddies instead of studying. Culbertson had volunteered for Vietnam, and was overjoyed with being posted to the 5th Marines. After some half-dozen patrols in Arizona Territory, the new point scout trainee still thought Vietnam was one hell of an adventure for a young buck ready to sow his oats. The deeply cut lines around Lafley's hollow eyes promised the new Marine grunt a brand-new perspective on the war's brutality and the cost of "staying alive." Lafley's thousand-yard stare could chill a new Marine to the bone. When the veteran cast his cold, dead eyes into your soul, young riflemen like PFC Culbertson didn't need to ask how it all came to pass. The stare grew harder and more lifeless with every mutilated brother Marine and each touch of the Grim Reaper's icy embrace.

Ron Willoughby turned and looked down the column of green-clad warriors as Foxtrot's lead platoon swung into view and paralleled Hotel. Nearly five hundred Marine infantrymen headed for the Thu Bon River and their rendezvous with Victor Charlie and his bloody-minded cousins from the north—the NVA. Willoughby cursed quietly to himself and snugged his free thumb up under his pack straps, relieving the weight and pressure for a moment. The Garand sniper rifle was no lightweight either, and along with two C-ration meals, two bandoleers of match ammunition, and entrenching tool, poncho, and extra socks, Willoughby figured he was humping about fifty to sixty pounds of gear through six inches of the slipperiest mud and slimiest rice paddy shit ever known to man or beast.

After four hours of march the company commanders ordered the platoon commanders to form their respective platoons into defensive perimeters for the night. Foxholes were immediately dug and machine guns were set in with fields of fire, carefully interlocked. The commanders got on the secure net to battalion headquarters and laid out the friendly coordinates for their lines so defensive artillery fires could be registered in the event of an enemy attack. Company 60mm mortars were set in, and 81mm mortars commanded by Headquarters and Service Companies providing nighttime illumination and protective fires for the perimeter. Ambushes were sent out in fire-team strength, and individual listening posts were established close to platoon lines to provide security along likely avenues of enemy approach.

Ron Willoughby and Vaughn Nickell went out with one ambush team to provide sniping cover as well as the ability to call in accurate artillery fire support. The snipers' duties were explicit, and no team was to engage an enemy force of platoon or company size by rifle fire. The snipers had been carefully picked, partly for their mathematical acumen, and were well-schooled in map reading and the techniques of calling in close artillery fire support against large enemy formations. Rumors floated around the grunt outfits about snipers who had shot up whole enemy rifle companies with bolt-action rifles. Anyone who had been in combat knew those rumors were the kind of bullshit that could get a sniper team killed if they were stupid enough to try something idiotic like that. In the Marine Corps, Ron Willoughby knew that killing Charlie was a team effort, and that a hell of a lot more VC got their passports to hell stamped courtesy of U.S. Marine artillery, the "King of Battle," than ever got shot to death by any sniper or grunt marksman.

As the ambush team moved out, Willoughby and Nickell felt reassured by the hard faces of Tim Kirby, John Jessmore, Luther Hamilton, John Lafley, and his rookie point scout apprentice, John Culbertson. An hour later the seven Marines scanned the fields leading toward the river, which lay a mile distant and wound through the jungle and rice fields like a giant green cobra. Each bend in the river offered sanctuary to the enemy. It was virtually impossible to predict when an enemy column might just march into view, only to disappear again into the protective cloak of the jungle. Willoughby reminded himself that this wild and dangerous country was Charlie's backyard, and Marines who made the mistake of taking extra chances went home early in a steel casket. This wasn't 1965, or even 1966, when small patrols could walk the countryside with relative safety. This was 1967, when more large engagements would be fought in I Corps than any other year of the Vietnam War. This was the year that the American Marine high command at II MAF would chase the Viet Cong regiments down in their own backyard and force them to stand and fight.

Willoughby tensed as the full realization of 2/5's mission hit home. This operation was the first round in a new campaign that would be fought tooth and nail to the bloody end against the Viet Cong and the new aggressors from North Vietnam. The first years of the war had just been a sideshow! This new offensive was for all the marbles. And it was a cold, hard fact that the professionals like Colonel William C. Airheart and his gunslingers, Captains Doherty and Burgett, would not come home without some serious enemy blood on their hands.

As the sun sank in a splash of golden fire into the river, a file of Vietnamese entered the long paddy dike system and walked at an angle toward the ambush site about a thousand meters to the west. Vaughn Nickell got his binoculars focused and glassed a group of farmers in black pajamas and white linen smocks. They looked like the local Viet Cong guerrillas who often guided main force and NVA ambush teams close to the Marine perimeters. The grunts took up their rifles, waiting for the file of VC to come into range. Neither Willoughby nor Nickell doubted that the hardcore grunt riflemen would kill the Vietnamese at the drop of a hat. Hell, no one doubted that any villagers along the bends of the river within the score of hostile villages like Cu Ban 4, La Bac 1 and 2, or La Thap 4, would gleefully aid the Communist effort to attack and destroy the Marine invaders. The grunts had seen so many of their brothers maimed and killed that they were pretty damn lax about who they shot, as long as they carried a weapon or threatened the security of the Marine operations.

Sergeant Casey came from a southern background where honor and fidelity were considered hallmarks of the warrior class. Obsolete in the vicious jungle war of Vietnam where the Geneva Convention was a joke, Casey had drilled his snipers on the value of what he called "righteous killing" as opposed to "wanton killing." Strong-minded as well as strong-armed, Casey had embedded his code of personal battlefield behavior in his snipers. Just like the personal ethos of Captains Doherty and Burgett, who never shrank from a fight but would never tolerate the killing of women or children. This war would be won by the Americans, Casey believed, because we fought harder and followed the rules of engagement, not because we were murderers like the Viet Cong and their henchmen, the North Vietnamese.

Vaughn Nickell spoke firmly as the grunts flipped off the safeties inside the trigger guards of their M-14 rifles: "Hold your fire boys. That file of gooks is only farmers. They got no weapons and there're two women in the group. If they don't come any closer, then we got to let 'em go!"

Several of the grunts snapped their safeties back on and looked at Vaughn like he was nuts. One hard Marine spoke for the grunts, saying, "You got the glasses my man! But for fifteen cents I say we should waste these assholes. They spy on us and tell the Viet Cong the distances to our perimeters so they can mortar the shit out of us come nightfall; hate these fuckers and nobody can convince me that any of 'em are worth shit."

Well, so much for the proprieties of war in Vietnam! Vaughn Nickell had saved the lives of a bunch of villagers he would never get to know. But the raw truth of the matter was that it was an even better bet that they were Viet Cong, and that by nightfall the mortar rounds would come tearing in Marine lines with a deadly accuracy that only spies could provide.

Ron Willoughby looked at the grunts as they placed their rifles back in their holes. He had no doubt that when the chance came, these men would kill the enemy like the Tartars of olden times and never bother to blink as the gruesome piles of dead stacked up.

Sources

"Down in the Shit": Excerpt from pp. 159–69 from *American Sniper* by Chris Kyle and Scott McEwen and Jim DeFelice. Copyright © 2012, 2013 by CT Legacy, LLC. Reprinted by permission of HarperCollins Publishers.

"Gunny Mitchell Comes to Casey's Aid": Excerpt from *13 Cent Killers: The 5th Marine Snipers in Vietnam* by John Culbertson, copyright © 2003 by John J. Culbertson. Used by permission of Presidio Press, an imprint of Random House, a division of Penguin Random House LLC. All rights reserved.

"It's Not about Killing, It's about Living, and Somehow I Lived" from *Snipers* by Lena Sisco, copyright © 2016. Used by permission of Globe Pequot/Lyons Press.

"Target Practice: 1918" from *The Plattsburgh Manual, A Handbook for Military Training* by Major O. O. Ellis, United States Infantry, and Major E. B. Garey, United States Infantry, copyright © 1918, The Century Company.

"The Hide Site: Three Stories" from *Sniper: American Single-Shot Warriors in Iraq and Afghanistan* by Gina Cavallaro with Matt Larsen © 2010. Used by permission of Globe Pequot/Lyons Press.

"The Long Shot" from *Long Rifle: A Sniper's Story in Iraq and Afghanistan* by Joe LeBleu copyright © 2009. Used by permission of Globe Pequot/Lyons Press.

"The Sniper in the Trenches" from *Sniping in France* by Major H. Hesketh-Prichard copyright © 1920. Hutchinson & Company.

"The Sharpshooters of Vermont: A Civil War Account" from *Vermont Riflemen in the War for the Union, 1861 to 1865* by Lieutenant Colonel William Y. W. Ripley copyright © 1883. Tuttle & Company.

"April Fool's Day" from *Shooter: An Autobiography of the Top-Ranked Marine Sniper* copyright © 2005 by Donald A. Davis. Reprinted by permission of St. Martin's Press, LLC. All rights reserved.

"The Nastiest Fight" from *Sniper: American Single-Shot Warriors in Iraq and Afghanistan* by Gina Cavallaro with Matt Larsen copyright © 2010. Used by permission of Globe Pequot/Lyons Press.

"Storm Clouds Gather over Go Noi Island" from *13 Cent Killers: The 5th Marine Snipers in Vietnam* by John Culbertson, copyright © 2003 by John J. Culbertson. Used by permission of Presidio Press, an imprint of Random House, a division of Penguin Random House LLC. All rights reserved.